# Notes of a Lost Pilot

JEAN BERAUD VILLARS, born in the outskirts of Paris in 1893, was educated in France, England, and Germany. In 1914 he was a cavalry officer and was wounded at the start of the war. An infantry volunteer in 1915, he was again wounded, this time more gravely. Transferred to aviation at the beginning of 1916, he was an observation pilot and then a pursuit pilot. In the spring of 1917, he was shot down in aerial combat, receiving a bullet in the foot. Several weeks later he returned to the front as commander of an escadrille where he was gravely wounded by D. C. A. (ground fire) which paralyzed his arm and he no longer flew. However, he would again be mobilized in an aviation headquarters in 1939-40.

Businessman, traveller, he wrote a number of historical works and a biography of Colonel Lawrence, which, translated into English, was published in London and in New York in 1959.

The Young Aviator

## BOOKS BY JEAN BERAUD VILLARS

Notes d'un pilote disparu — Hachette, 1918

Timour — Éditions de France, 1936. Épuisé.

La Nouvelle Hespéride — Éditions de France, 1938. Épuisé

L'empire de Gâo.
   Un état soudanais aux XV et XVI siècles — Plon, 1942
   [Prix Thérouanne de l'Académie Française]
   [Prix Lyautey de l'Académie des Sciences Coloniales]

Les Tourages au pays du Cid
   Les invasions almoravides en Espagne aux XI
   et XII siècles — Plon, 1946

Les Normands en Méditerranée — Albin Michel, 1951
   [Prix Née de l'Académie Française]

Le colonel Lawrence ou la recherche de l'Absolu
— Albin Michel, 1955

English Translation *T. E. Lawrence; or, The Search For The Absolute*
London, Sidgwick and Jackson, 1958

L'Islam d'hier et de toujours — B. Arthaud, 1969

# NOTES OF

# a lost pilot

by
Jean Beraud Villars

Translated and edited with foreword and notes,
by Stanley J. Pincetl, Jr., & Ernest Marchand
Illustrations by Charles Faust

Archon Books               1975

*Library of Congress Cataloging in Publication Data*

Béraud-Villars, Jean Marcel Eugène.
Notes of a lost pilot.

Translation of Notes d'un pilote disparu.
1. European war, 1914-1918—Aerial operations,
French. 2. European War, 1914-1918—Personal narra-
tives, French. 3. Béraud-Villars, Jean Marcel Eugène.
I. Title.
D603.B4713        940.4′49′44  [B]        74-2112
ISBN 0-208-01437-3

Original French language edition first
published 1918 [© 1918 Hachette]
Translation of revised manuscript first published
1975 as an Archon Book, an imprint of
The Shoe String Press, Inc.
Hamden, Connecticut 06514

© 1975 by Stanley J. Pincetl

To

MARCEL BARTHE

Cadet Officer of the 27th Alpine

and

ROBERT SENECHAL

Pursuit pilot

killed by the enemy

# Contents

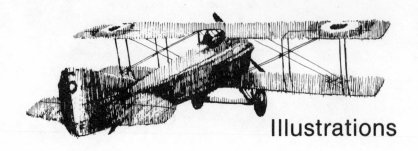

# Illustrations

# Foreword

Among the most romantic figures whose valor was challenged in individual combat were the aviators of the First World War. Certainly this was the stuff to stimulate writers—and it did. But of the hundreds (or thousands) of accounts, by actual combatants, of flying in the War of 1914-1918, few in any language are of real literary worth, few of the stature of Cecil Lewis's *Saggitarius Rising*, written years after the end of the war.

For the French, who suffered the worst blood-letting of any nation in the First World War, books of any kind on flying are extremely rare. Indeed, what we know of French aviation in this country comes almost entirely from the large number of books by and about the Americans who flew for France in the Lafayette Escadrille and flying corps or other French units. The major work translated into English from the French is that of the foremost French ace, René Fonck, whose book was written after the war. Investigation shows that the total accounts by French flying personnel probably consist of only three journals, three volumes of recollections, three of letters, and four novels. Of these, one is clearly superior by almost any standard, but it was also the most mysterious. Titled

*Notes d'un pilote disparu* (Hachette, 1918), it was presented by a Lieutenant Marc,* who states that he gathered the random notes of a fallen comrade and published the work, which, incidentally, was heavily censored. Not only does it contain a detailed description, by an acute and sensitive observer, of the character and life of the French reconnaissance and pursuit pilots from Verdun to August, 1917, but it is also a fine piece of literature, obviously written by a man of culture and education.

The challenges confronting the translators were first of all to try to find the real author of the work, and secondly to try to restore the censored passages. A letter to the publisher brought very surprising results, for the author of this book, Monsieur J. Beraud Villars, responded to our inquiry and is alive and well, as his Preface to this translation proves. He has told why he published his *Notes* under the name of Lieutenant Marc, and has given us the opportunity to restore most of the censored parts of the work by furnishing a copy of the uncensored typescript, though for one reason or another—the lapse of time, the mislaying or loss of papers—a few passages are still missing. He has also furnished many names of actual people and units involved, as indicated in the notes, and he has been more than helpful with problems of translation, in making intelligible the slang used in French aviation of the day.

---

*Monsieur Villars explains that the name Marc for the ostensible author of these notes was suggested by the fact that his father was named Marcel and that he himself is named Jean Marcel. The name is traditional in his family, and was later bestowed on his own son.

We are very happy to have "found" him after these lost years, and are extremely grateful for his cooperation. We hope that our translation will make a contribution to an area of the literature of flying in the First World War hitherto unknown to an American audience.

To Professor Jean Guiguet, Director of American Studies at the University of Aix, our obligations are also very great. He has guided us through many of the subtleties of the French language and has saved us from a number of errors, though he cannot be held to account for any that may remain. And our special thanks go to F. T. Quiett, former RCAF pilot and retired senior pilot USAR, who has advised us on a number of technical points concerning aviation in the First World War, a subject of his continuing interest. The illustrator of this volume is Charles M. Faust, San Diego artist, bomber pilot in the Second World War, with a special interest in the aircraft of the First World War. He is a board member of the International Aerospace Hall of Fame, located in San Diego.

Censored passages here restored are enclosed in square brackets. Notes supplied by the author bear his initials, J.B.V.; notes unsigned are by the translators.

Stanley J. Pincetl, Jr.
Ernest Marchand

San Diego State University

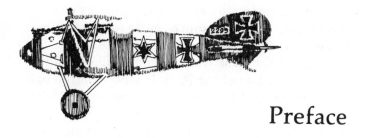

# Preface

The title of this book and its last pages contain an inaccuracy: the major personage of the account did not disappear, for he is writing these lines.

This was a subterfuge rather than a deception. In 1917, as a member of the Armed Forces, I did not have the right to print a book without submitting it to my superiors. Now my book contained rather lively criticisms and its printing doubtless would not have been authorized. I published it under a pseudonym and as a posthumous work, the pages written on my knees in a hospital bed, after I had been gravely wounded.

Except for this inaccuracy, I affirm that all of the facts related are exact, happened to me personally, that I have not romanced, or exaggerated anything, but rather softened certain episodes which were too shocking.

After half a century, it is with some emotion that, rereading my own work, I have recalled the youthful silhouettes of my companions, of whom so many have been devoured by Moloch. One does not stir with impunity memories at once so distant and so near.

The aviators of 1914-1918 flew machines of wood and canvas, they had no parachutes, many of them burned in the air. Their comrades of more recent conflicts had much more perfected machines, but their risks were clearly the same. The aviators of the first war resembled like brothers the pursuit pilots of the R. A. F. who won the battle of Britain, the American carrier pilots who, over the Coral Sea, went beyond the point of no return, the French aviators of the last hopeless combats of June, 1940.

It is a profession that forges men, but it is a certain kind of men who choose this profession.

I do not think that the reader will find in this work an exaltation of chauvinism, nor a blind praise of the profession of arms. He will discover, on the contrary, some bitterness behind a recital deliberately light-hearted. For the air combatant, the joke, cynicism, joyful sarcasm in regard to the commander, are the indispensable antidotes in maintaining the morale of men daily exposed to the dangers of anti-aircraft artillery, enemy pursuit and accident, who submit to being fair game and who treat other aviators as young as they, likewise.

To risk one's life day after day has never been a pleasant experience. All of those who find themselves in front of the wrong end of a machine gun in action have known anguish and fear. Novelists and journalists of propaganda who say the contrary are either imbeciles or liars or both at the same time.

But still, neither a people nor a civilization can survive if citizens do not observe the simple and painful virtues of a soldier.

J.B.V.

Pilot Lieutenant X. . . . of escadrille N.705 left on patrol the 6th of August, 1917, did not return to his field.

His two companions in combat lost sight of him crossing a layer of fog. Artillery observers described a dog fight at 17 hundred hours between several German aircraft and a Spad which fell in flames near the forest of Houthulst.

On the table of the lost pilot were found a large number of pages of manuscript and an unsealed letter dated that same day.

A part of these notes is printed here—a pilot's journal, impressions hastily written, reflections on events, things and people, all in a chronology unfortunately not precise because the sheets were thrown pell-mell in the box which contained them.

We have suppressed all which related to the private life of the pilot and too violent criticism against persons and institutions.

# Part One

*F.00 at Verdun**

---

*Maurice-Farman Escadrille 44. Insignia: Inverted Double
Horseshoes.

# I
# Verdun, May, 1916

Neither at the Marne nor in Flanders nor in the offensives in Champagne in 1915 did aviation have a role so important, a task so difficult, or days so tragic as at Verdun, starting with the German attacks at the end of February.

Three or four escadrilles defended and reconnoitered the original Verdun sector. They were surprised by the offensive and were manhandled and decimated in a few days. Since then all the aerial units available on our front were sent here, as much to seize control of the air from the enemy as to fill the gaps in our effectives from daily losses which were greater than aviation has ever had before.

All bits of news complacently designed to flatter our national vanity and to quiet our concern; all the erroneous information coming from ignorant or interested people, all the poorly informed newspaper articles have brought acceptance of the axiom that our aviation has an absolute and definitive superiority over that of the enemy. We lived by this illusion, but things have taken place rapidly and brutally which have imposed on us a more realistic and a more severe view of our true situation.

We were obliged to draw up our balance sheet

to see just where we stood: insufficient effectives, a personnel whose young and eager elements are mixed with tired out pilots, equipment of very uneven worth and generally inferior to that of the enemy, that is to say, excellent single-seat Nieuports, two-seat Nieuports scarcely adequate, mediocre twin-engine Caudrons (G.4) and finally the Farmans and Voisins. These latter are hard to maneuver, slow, vulnerable from the rear because of the position of the motor. They have become the defenseless prey, "Gefressenes Futter," of the German pilots. [One cannot understand why they are not yet replaced by new models. The negligence, the complaisance which has allowed these outmoded types, incompatible with the present war, to be kept till 1916, is being paid for today with terrible losses.]

To help the Nieuports which were given too much to do with reduced effectives, groups of twin-engine planes were formed to protect the range finding, liaison and photographic missions, but in vain. These G.4 exert themselves to the utmost, accept combat and have downed some Boches, taking a beating. But they cannot contain an enemy aviation which is aggressive, numerous and well organized.

Briefly then, despite the efforts, the courage and the energy of our escadrilles, we have not succeeded in dominating the Boche. Our observation planes of the Army Corps are denied access to the German lines while the Fokkers, the Rumplers and the Aviatiks daily fly over our trenches, spot our positions and knock down our Voisins and Farmans right up to our batteries.

Our escadrille, the F.00, was dormant and inactive for eight months, attached to a corps of the army of Champagne. This corps, called to Verdun, brings us along with it to the great affray. The enervating calm of a rest area is over for us. We joyfully join the best of our army on this front which promises limitless dangers and honors.


. . . 17 May. We leave N. . . , in Champagne, to meet at Vadelaincourt. The observers go by car; the pilots with their mechanics fly by way of Ta-hure, Massiges, the large open expanse of the Argonne, Vauquois and Avocourt.

Of the twelve of us, only Sergeant Buette has a breakdown and remains stuck near Sainte-Mene-hould; the eleven others reach their destination, but just as I arrive one of the last, Adjutant Le Boeuf, who precedes me, overshoots the runway and flips over in the ruts without hurting himself, but with great injury to his Farman, which is com-pletely smashed up.

Disoriented on this large field where there are canvas hangars everywhere, I taxi toward the first group of Bessonneaus.* The mechanics I question know nothing about F.00. They make a few vague signs and leave me to my fate. I get the same lack of interest from everyone. I finally see a yellow-orange pennant. My comrades have found the corner designated for us and are al-ready undressing.

The captain is there, having arrived yesterday in a touring car. He looks around, fusses, fidgets, runs in all directions. He has his cap on the back of his head, his eternal cane, and his no less eter-nal little rain cape; he becomes irritable, is in de-

---

*A canvas hangar to hold four to six planes.

spair. The army air branch bewails lack of space, lodges him at the worst end of the field, gives him Bessonneaus with holes where the planes will be wet, and lodges his personnel in an unfinished roofless hut.

The wind from the west, which gave us such a push during our trip, brings a downpour which caps the climax of the misery and disorder. The chief spills his troubles to me and tells me of the latest disasters; the photography truck has broken down at Revigny; three tractors have gone astray; Max,* his right hand man, has not yet arrived, and the office portable desk is lost. He leaves me to rush off to a Captain, head of services, to ask him for a thousand indispensable things which will of course be refused to us.

The disorder of our arrival mingles in the general disorder of the camp and is increased by it. Without adversely affecting the units stationed at Brocourt, Froidos, Julvécourt, Souilly, Autrécourt, Ancemont, a great number of escadrilles have piled up on the Lemmes-Vadelaincourt field: escadrilles of Voisins, Farmans, Nieuports, G.4's, mingling their planes, their tractors, their trailers, their touring cars, their temporary tents, their personnel huts, their armories, their radio and photo shacks, their rolling kitchens.

Newly arrived in an unknown sector, under unknown chiefs, we wander in the mud hunting for shelter until, with comradely help, each of us finds in a friendly or obliging unit, a supper, a chair, a bed, a place as fourth for a bridge game in the evening.

F.00 is the escadrille of the ——th Army Corps,

*Lt. and then Capt. Marc Sourdillon, who survived the war. J. B. V.

Arrival at Vadelaincourt

that is to say, that it provides the photos of the sector, and if necessary, assures the aerial liaison between the infantry and the commander, finally directs the fire of its heavy and field artillery.

It is made up of flying personnel of twelve pilots (one captain, one lieutenant, one second lieutenant, nine non-commissioned officers) and twelve observers, all officers; a non-flying personnel called ground crew, a hundred mechanics, chauffeurs, gunsmiths, photographers, radio operators. Add three dogs, a little barn owl, a magpie, and you will know all about escadrille F.00, which a yellow-orange pennant with a blue star distinguishes from the others.

Our chief is Captain Pardirel, an engineering officer who entered aviation in 1914; he is energetic, authoritarian, brisk, and an organizer. Each must submit willingly or unwillingly to his rather tyrannical authority and give in to his long experience. He has things well under control and wants to remain the only boss. His headstrong and combative nature pushes him sometimes to achieve cooperation of various branches, accompanied by the most frightful dissensions; but these conflicts always end happily, for the chief has the gift of making all those who have relations with him see his way.

De Montault, the second lieutenant, comes from the hussars. Physically he has the appearance of a hard-knotted grapevine; his overflowing energy drives him ceaselessly and pushes him, when he cannot fly, to make interminable excursions on foot, by bicycle, or even provision trucks. Mentally, a Bohemian and gay originality, quite unstudied, colors all his actions and his words.

Our other comrades are artillerymen. I had a

prejudice against artillerymen which dated from peacetime. The dragoons among whom I served did not like them; was it rivalry between a sporting and a technical branch, jealousy, political differences? I don't know. It was necessary to maintain esprit de corps and the rivalry which resulted from it, since this made up most of provincial garrison life.

Since then I have seen and known artillerymen; I have lived with them. On rainy days we have played bridge, flown among cannon bursts on sunny days; waited with them the time for liaison with the infantry, shivered with them on early autumn mornings watching the fog lift; in twenty combats an artilleryman held the machine gun while I piloted. We have also bickered, argued; we have bravely spoken our minds, which was not always very pleasant. Still, after months of life in common, I value, esteem, and like the artillerymen, judging them by the twelve aerial observers who were my companions and my friends in the F.00.

First of all they are usually recruited from among the students of the Centrale, of the X,* or of the School of Mines. This gives the artillerymen a homogeneous intellectual background which is superior to that of the other branches.

One can talk, discuss, learn, raise tactical, technical or professional questions with artillerymen. They are always capable of giving an opinion, often an opinion which is too theoretical, but intelligent, on all sorts of subjects, whether it is a question of armament of an aircraft or the construction of a hut.

*École Polytechnique

And furthermore artillerymen are brave. Those who say the contrary have not seen the busy hives of range finding and photography at Verdun and the Somme where "the old range finders of the 120 longs"* took off from fifty Bessonneaus in all weather, flipping over on landing, cracking up, getting themselves shot down by the Boches, by cannon or machine guns, flying in wretched crates, always working, dogged, indefatigable.

They have no more desire to get themselves killed than any others. But they have a great concern for the work to be done, and desire to finish it cost what it may; an idea of duty, strong and simple, maintains them more than swagger, which is not characteristic of these practical and objective mathematicians.

Going into action is the only way to get results; they employ this means, then, in default of another, as the result is indispensable.

In the F.00 we do not know the classic disagreements between pilots and observers. Certainly many among the observers would like to fly a plane and this is a very legitimate desire. I do not understand why they do not let a large number of them into flight schools; instructed, they would make at the same time perfect technical and tactical escadrille chiefs.

Moreover, their role grows larger and larger and they are daily taking a more active part in the command. The period is ending when the pilots, jealous of their prerogatives, held them at arm's length, humiliated them and treated them as baggage and poor relations. It has been under-

*Seven- or eight-inch guns.

stood that the efficiency of a range-finding and liaison escadrille depends almost uniquely on the worth of its observers.

Nevertheless, their situation is not yet what it should be. Perhaps it is feared that once installed in the escadrilles of the Army Corps the artillerymen would expel all other elements and keep command of them for themselves. This challenges certain ambitions. It is logical, however, that the units whose work is almost entirely the work of artillery should be under the control of the professionals of the discipline rather than of cavalrymen or infantrymen.

In any event, there is the best of feeling in F.00 between pilots and observers. We ignore foolish arguments and inadmissible rivalry between people called upon to live and fight and die side by side.

Except for the chief, who is thirty or so, there is none among us more than twenty-five years of age. Not one of us is married, and each operates with the freedom and cheerfulness of youth which nothing can restrain, and the F.00 is certainly the most alert, the gayest, the most homogeneous outfit that can be found at the moment when they are fated for this great adventure.


Everything settles down, says military wisdom, more trite but more succinct than that of nations. The tractors arrive one by one. The lost and the laggards assemble. We are finally given the necessary barracks and hangars. Sergeant Buette, who had broken down at Sainte-Menehould, will rejoin us tomorrow and the office portable desk has been found. The captain has calmed down and sees order restored to his unit, which yesterday was dispersed. As for us, up to our ears in mud, we help park the tractors and the trailers, which sink to their hubs, between the two Bessonneaus. At the same time we look stealthily at the sky to see if it is clearing enough to let us take a first look at the sector.

About two o'clock, thanks to a blue patch, I take off with Max. In ten minutes we have reached our altitude and are over the lines. The Verdun front extends before us.

We thought we knew what a shell-holed region was, a landscape of attack, but the modest upheaval of Champagne was nothing compared to the desolation which we have before our eyes.

Beyond the dense row of observation balloons, so close that in places they seem to touch each other, the earth is pock-marked with shell holes which, at first spaced out, finish by merging with each other. For twenty kilometers in length and ten in depth the soil is an open wound, the color of clay and fresh earth; the villages are destroyed, broken up; the forts are nothing more than geometric phantoms eaten out by shell craters. The pool of Vaux is but a vaguely outlined and muddy puddle; the streams without a bed lose themselves, and the woods, chewed up, slashed, destroyed, scarcely shade the soil with their lamentable trunks.

The two infantries are lost in this lunary landscape. Without shelter, without trenches, cut off during the day from all liaison with the rear, the infantrymen are lying in the shell holes following the imprecise line which the combat changes daily.

At the time we are flying, a relative calm reigns on the right bank. Only a few shells burst from time to time. But suddenly on hill 304 and Mort-

Homme, smoke and dust stirred up by the bombardment show that the enemy is preparing an assault or a surprise attack.

Contrary to what would happen in calm sectors where the defense against aviation has time to be minutely organized, we receive neither rifle nor cannon shots although we are flying at only two or three thousand feet. On the other hand, the front is closely patrolled by enemy pursuit planes; scarcely arrived at our first lines, we see fast crates descend to meet us, approach resolutely, fire, and we are obliged to give way. That is nothing which should surprise us: those who have been long in the sector have warned us that at Verdun Farmans cannot cross the trenches without being exposed to the hazards of an unequal combat. Up to our lines a great number of F.40's have been attacked and brought down and prudence tells us not to climb above 3500 or 4500 feet during our missions. As to the photographers who have to fly over the enemy zone, they have to choose the proper moment, which is very rare, when the Boche barrage is slack; even then they act at their risk and peril.

For quite some time Max studies the sector where we will have to work from now on. On the terrain levelled by shells, landmarks are missing; all is confused in a desert of uniformity and the eye is lost among the ridges and ravines which are equally eaten out, stripped and naked.

Suddenly, just as we start to return, an unexpected nervousness runs through the sector; two batteries first of all start to fire; the others become active and fire in their turn, all the line is afire; and when we leave, the artillery duel rolls anew on the whole length of the front.

A telephone call informs the squadron* that Sergeant Buette and his mechanic, leaving yesterday evening from Sainte-Menehould, had their motor quit on take-off, hit a line of trees and were killed.

Thus, the first two casualties which the campaign of Verdun will have cost the F.00 will have been these two comrades, struck down by the most wretched chance, without a fight, far from the lines on a strange field.

# II

Each evening, the chief makes out the service sheet for the next day, based on the choice of Max, who picks out the observers, and me, who designates the pilots. "Such and such pilot with such and such an observer. Range finding on a certain point, or liaison, or photo." Thus each knows what he should do the following day, studies his mission, picks his time, gets information by telephone. The work done, he is free to do as he likes.

But we have not a moment to lose; when the sky allows, each crew flies twice a day:

"Where is our infantry?" screams the Army Corps. We know nothing about it; we are told it is holding the Lamy trench and communication

*The translators have used indifferently throughout the terms *escadrille and squadron,* sometimes preserving the French word (equally current in English), sometimes rendering it *squadron.* The composition of these units varies as to number of men and planes.

trench 3A, but in reality, as trench and communication trench, nothing. All of that has been long wiped out and there remain only shell holes. When liaison officers are sent, they march four or five hours by compass, in pot holes up to their eyes, not knowing where they are and end by falling over prone poilus in the shell holes who say to them: "Don't go any farther, you are going to catch it; here it is us, there it is the Boches." And the liaison officers return without knowing anything more. This is a poor way to find a line. Only planes can straighten that out. "Send the planes. . . ."

And the crates take off. They make their presence known by flares, and infantrymen, when they are not too frozen or wet, mark out their lines by conventional signals.

This is infantry liaison. We do this during a period of calm as well as during an attack to mark the successive progression of our assault waves.

Range finding is another thing. When the objectives are beyond the sight of the ground observers and observation balloons, the aircraft itself becomes at the same time elevated and mobile observer; it communicates with the battery by radio; the battery answers by canvas panels disposed according to an agreed upon code.

"Too short, too long, to the right, on target," says one. "I am ready, understood, I have fired, wait five minutes," answers the other. When the shells are about on target, the battery fires by salvos of twenty or thirty of which the plane has only to correct the general grouping.

Actually, things take place less simply. All sorts of incidents hold up range finding; artillerymen dawdle, messages are poorly received, the artillery

Briefing

captain hangs on to his firing range which he feels is right and will not change it according to the indications of the aviator, or again refuses to fire in order not to be seen by a Nieuport which flies over and which he takes for an enemy aircraft.

Impatient, the observer becomes agitated in his cockpit, leans over the side, rattles the key of his transmitter, swears like a trooper, while the pilot, who has nothing to do, goes around in circles watching for German planes, looks at his panel clock and finds that the time passes very slowly.

The operation would last indefinitely if the far-sighted builders had not limited the gas in our tanks to three hours and a half. Eternal hours during which guns of armored cars blast at us with white, greenish or black shell bursts, while barrage planes resort to clever tactics to surprise us at the corner of a cloud and try to shoot us down. Hours which have their good moments when at times the battery or ammunition dump which we shell blows up and burns and we can console ourselves for our troubles, thinking of the German artillerymen smothered in their shelter or blown up by the explosion.

. . . May. Basil* takes me on my first range finding over Verdun. After several days of bad weather, the sky is superb. All the escadrilles, kept in the hangars during the rains, take out their aircraft. Vadelaincourt is full of activity. Twin engines, Voisins, Nieuports, Farmans take off and land. At take off it is necessary to keep

*Lt., then Capt., Cyril Lebarbu, killed in 1917 as commander of a bombing escadrille. J. B. V.

your eyes open not to run into a buddy or to be hit in the flank by an excited young pilot in landing. Wrecked crates cover the field with their remains; the hen coops (Farmans) break their wings with the characteristic sound of a crushed match box; the twin props turn over with dignity; the Nieuports stand on their noses or somersault to come to rest with their wheels in the air with the funny and vexed look of a large insect on its back.

The blockhouse at which we are aiming is really taking a beating; the Boche commander must have received all of the command post beams on his head when the target was hit at the eighth round.

We are obliged to remain within our lines. The Boche is aggressive. Our pursuit planes, whose pilots fly two or three times a day, cannot contain him. Perhaps our patrols lack cohesion, but in any case the Germans have a large numerical superiority in combat aircraft. Unless the Farmans want to be dangerously attacked they must be very careful and stay at home. One of them allowed itself to be attacked at 7500 feet near Souville; a Boche single-seater dived on it and we saw the F.40, its pilot killed or its controls cut, fall wing over wing. It turned over with wheels in the air at about 1500 feet and suddenly a body went straight down, then the aircraft crashed on the roofs of Verdun.

Yet, in certain places, the French planes are so numerous that the slightest inattention would risk bringing a collision. We are two orange pennants over the lines. Adjutant Le Boeuf, piloting Mario, is range finding at the same time we are for a 155. At times we fly toward each other and, our speed doubled, we pass each other like arrows with a swiftness which seems to make us dizzy. Sometimes for an instant we fly side by side. Mario waves at me with a hand swollen by his enormous glove and his Farman looks like a large immobile bird inexplicably tied to a string, ridiculous and pretentious with its feet tucked under its belly.

Le Boeuf has, in accord with his name, the ox, a lack of suppleness, a bluff and direct courage. He flies in a straight line and for nothing in the world would he do a flashy zoom or a vertical bank, but flies through the cannon shells with an Olympian tranquility and attacks the Boche like an antique hero. We recognize him from way off because his rear stabilizer is decorated with a delicate picture of a butterfly.

We return, leaving Mario behind us in difficulty with his transmitter. The sun is going down and three Nieuports leave for their last patrol. Basil rolls in his antenna and standing in the cockpit, leaning on his gun turret, sings the great aria of I Pagliacci* with gestures, an artistic performance which I unfortunately do not appreciate because of the deafening noise of my 130 hp.

Each evening two of us are taken by car to Army Corps and to the artillery to find out what work has been accomplished and to take orders for the next day.

The liaison route. The desolated landscape. The faubourg of Verdun where a reservist armed with a little flag imposes order on the eternal passage of troops, autos, and vehicles. The lines bottle up, dust accumulates in the folds of our uniforms, powders our faces, covers our eyelids and moustaches, and we wait for hours between

*In the French, Paillasse.

teams of frightened horses which endanger our fenders, and a relief which passes trampling like sheep.

We are going to see our general staff of the Army Corps which preceded us here while the bad weather kept us in Champagne. We bring them the first information about the lines and the emplacements of the .batteries, the first photos of the sector where the divisions have already been wallowing for a week.

We are received with open arms as people who are needed. Without our precious help, we are told, the Army Corps is like a child without its mother. We knew this; the general does not ignore the advice of his squadron chief. Two or three times a week our chief has to bring him, not only information within his province, but pointers on general politics and on the situation of the allied armies on all the fronts—scuttlebutt gathered at times in gossiping in the very offices of the Army Corps.

Far removed from the Army Corps, in a village shelled daily by enemy cannon, with demolished houses, with empty streets which we pass grazing the walls, we discover the two dugouts of the front line division and the heavy artillery of the sector. In these underground places officers and men write, work, and telephone. These troglodytes deal with the business at hand and then try to interest us in their concern about the strength of their shelter.

Are they visible from the air? Can enemy planes spot them, and by deadly aim, hit the division headquarters? They beg us to take photos, numerous photos, to verify the camouflage. We promise the photos.

The return. Night falls. In the sky, the comrades who return drop down near us, wave at our car and will be in five minutes where we will not be for an hour.

The freshness of the wind makes us regret the coat we disdained. Along the road a truck driver who has broken a wheel in a rut and whom the line of others has abandoned, gets out, sees the disaster, and without enthusiasm takes out his tool box and his crescent wrench, feels alone and depressed.

. . . June. Under a burning sky, under a torrid sun, Vadelaincourt shrivels up. We watch the hot air dancing on the cracked soil. The last pilots coming in yell to us that they have had their hands full and that they have never taken such a buffeting.

As we sit down to attack the hors-d'oeuvre of lunch, the telephone demands a plane for an urgent spotting and Delame gets up, drags me to the chore of flying at high noon.

Outside it is stifling and even my dog dares not leave the shelter of the tent and risk sunstroke to accompany me to the planes. In the hangar, Octave, my mechanic, almost naked, is dripping while he buttons me in my esquimau dress where I feel I am expiring; he grabs the propeller: "Ready?" he cries. "Ready!" and we taxi off in a whirling cloud of dust.

I take off. Our comrades, napkins on their arms, salute our departure and we are in the sickening agitation of this unstable and warm air. A draft takes us and we ascend like an elevator. Another current sends us toward the ground. The wind which blows hot on our faces pushes us to the left, to the right, to the edge of a side slip and the ailerons refuse to stablize us. I work like a trooper to maintain my large crate in a line of flight. Sweat stings my eyes, my uniform suffocates me and I cannot gain any altitude. Finally at 3600 feet the air is suddenly calm and a breath of light fresh air slides between our teeth like a glass of cold water.

But over the lines, the vigilant Boche force us to descend into the hot cauldron at 2100 or 2400 feet and the turbulence shakes us up anew for the two hours our mission lasts. As we return, we receive our final roughing up from the ammunition dump of a 155 on the slope of Froideterre which a German shell blew up below us. We fly through a column of smoke and explosions, a few of which send pieces through our canvas. Below there must be a terrible mess among the artillerymen. As we fly along the Meuse, we continue to see the smoke of the explosions which succeed one another.

We land. After the fatigue of several hours of flying, I never land without apprehension on this field, cut-up and full of holes.

My mechanic, who runs to hold on to the wing and to lead me to the hangars, has eyes swollen with sleep—he has slept, the dog; all the field has slept while we danced over the lines. The German artillerymen, incidentally, also were taking a siesta, for we did not receive a cannon shot.

The mechanics help us to get out, guiding our stiff legs to the footsteps. We take off our flying togs, whose fur suffocates us. They have every concern for us, for they are good fellows. My "first" has a bizarre Flemish name which I always forget and I call him familiarly by his first name, Octave. His helper, my "second," is called

Petitcygne (Little Swan). One can forget Poten-
hem or Vespermesch, but not Petitcygne and
nobody ignores this big fellow so delicately named.

We eat alone. One by one our comrades leave
for their missions and we sleep half naked,
sprawled on our beds until the calm of evening,
until sunset, which reddens the Argonne.

The work is finished; smoking and talking
about the flights, we watch Mario fly a kite whose
tail is stabilized by multicolored tracts "AN DIE
DEUTSCHEN SOLDATEN," a remainder of a
package which the squadron the other day threw
over the lines. These tracts strongly advised the
"Deutschen Soldaten" to come eat the white
bread of captivity, but they did not want to listen
and attacked anew near Douaumont.

Basil makes a hammock; Max teases the dogs;
as for the captain, he is in deep conversation with
an infantry major who asks him if the Farman is
a combat aircraft and why we do not purge the
sky of the Boches who dishonor it.

# III

. . . June. For ten days it has been fine and
warm. Each morning, the first among us who
gets up faces toward the west and "looks at the
Argonne." Looking at the Argonne is a conse-
crated rite. "Can you see it?" cries the chorus of
fliers who are still in bed. "It is visible!" answers
the coryphée who is usually in his pajamas, and
the tent of the squadron fills with the noise of

pilots and observers who get up to go to work. If he answers: "It is not visible," the occupants of the tent continue to sleep quietly, for they know that the sky is covered and the ground fog is not yet dissipated.

Actually, when the weather is fine for everyone else, it can be deplorable for the aviators. Even when the sky is blue, the ground is sometimes covered with a layer of mist which prevents us from seeing. This is the barrier of fog which, when we get through at about 5500 or 6000 feet, takes on the aspect of a grey blue sea under which the ground is effaced; and if we fly low, dominates us and seems like an opaque wall against which we will collide.

So each morning when we can see the Argonne (and we see it every day in this season) the crews leave. We all fly at least once a day. Since the infantry liaison is idle and since de Montault reserves photography for himself, range-finding is our chief duty.

One range finding a day, that's a bit monotonous. It is believed that our life is all freedom and fancy. Actually, we have our turn to take, a daily mission to perform at a designated hour, weather permitting, and we find ourselves over the lines with the punctuality of a sentry who comes to mount his guard.

A range finding, when the artillerymen work well, when we do not have any radio or motor trouble, lasts three to three and a half hours. It is hard work. It requires a great effort of will, of attention and endurance to remain for three hours with your hand on the controls and attached to your seat, like an oarsman in the galleys. To this immobility add, to tire us out, mental strain, constant menace of planes and cannon, variations of temperature, differences of pressure due to the altitude.

The chief does all he can to keep us from flying twice. One outing is enough; we step out of the plane considerably beaten, with smarting eyes, a stiff back and empty head. Waiting for the time when the liaison which will send us forty kilometers by car in the dust and confusion of the roads of Verdun, we slouch on our beds, shaken up every five minutes by the telephone, the hateful telephone, and so fagged out that we have neither the desire nor the time to read or to write.

But who can complain of having a painful task in this corner of the front where everyone, from the smallest to the greatest, suffers, wears himself out and gets himself killed.

Our work is monotonous only because fatigue robs us of the faculty of emotion and the idea of the picturesque, for everyday brings us its adventure and drama.

There are incidents which are personal to us, combats, shell splinters in the wings, the plane we risk colliding with in midair, the danger of a motor failure, range finding which succeeds or fails. Also there is what we see on the ground; comrades who are shot down by a shell or by a Boche, wounded, who use their last strength to return to land in front of the Bessonneaus and who, once there, pale and drawn, can no longer talk or get out of the cockpit; the crew which cries on landing: "There were three fires during my scuffle and I fired ten effective rounds"; another which cries, "That bunch of knotheads! They did not fire ten rounds and during that time I almost got shot down by two little Aviatiks from the left bank";

the fighters who return half crazy with excitement and tell the assembled crowd: "I shot him from three quarters to the rear after a steep climb and he started to catch fire . . ."; and the two Nieuports which we saw land side by side this morning, a pilot crying: "Good Lord, I got two, two with seven shots!" and the other, whose lower wing, half cut-off by a shell, vibrated, fluttered, almost detached from the fuselage: "I've never been so scared!"

Today Basil and I, during the spotting of a 120 long, tangled with two enemy two-seaters which attacked us at about 6600 feet as we were pushing toward our objective. We were seriously engaged and I have never seen so clearly the black crosses on the fuselage and on the wings. These crosses when seen close up on an enemy plane, make a strong and bizarre impression, difficult to express, as all those who have fought in the air will recall. Perhaps this impression comes because sight of these crosses is accompanied by that of a machine gun which sprays you with incendiary shells at four or five hundred feet.

The Boches, slow old fellows of the L. V. G. type, circled around us like big fish, not very adroit. They obviously did not want to get too close to us and as they have only one machine gun in the rear, they were obliged to pass along our flank to fire on us. Basil took aim, at ease and standing upright in the cockpit, and his calm was contagiously relaxing. Everything went off well. After several passes the Boches drew off leaving a few bullet holes in our wings that we might tell a boastful tale to our comrades.

But one should not be too flippant. If one has to deal with a pilot who is a bit aggressive, and who knows how to maneuver his crate, the adventure will inevitably take a bad turn. Many have been the victims who thought they had a victim.

[To fight against the Boches in a Farman presently in service is to put all the odds against you. Moral strength will not be enough if the instrument which you are using breaks up in your hands at the critical moment.

[The Farman is slow. That is a first weakness. In a fight, its adversaries circle around it, avoiding its fire, catch it when it flees, escape it when it wants to attack.

[The Farman is badly balanced. While other planes in service, Nieuport, Caudron, Sopwith, left to themselves fly in normal position, in a nose dive if the motor is cut, in horizontal flight at full power, the Farman must be piloted without a second's inattention, for once put in the wrong position, it cannot be corrected. It stays on one wing, in a spin or on its back until the final crash. The pilot thus cannot do any acrobatics with the plane during the course of a combat.

[The Farman is not solid. As soon as its speed goes beyond a modest limit (between 180 and 200 kilometers an hour), its wings break up under the pressure of the air. This accident has taken place twenty times. We dare not dive a bit steeply, do a reversal, or a spin, in fear of seeing the crate fold like a pocket book while the fuselage falls with the motor. An eventuality infinitely demoralizing for the pilots.

[Finally, and especially, the Farman is badly protected; the motor and the wings being placed behind the passengers, the machine gunner cuts the longeron and the propellor if he fires to the rear, and the Boche has only to put himself under the stabilizer of the crate to knock it down without receiving a bullet.

[Why do we still have the Farmans? What shady conduct of suppliers and of builders! What incompetence and what negligence of technical service obliges us after two years of campaign to fight in machines clearly inferior to all the enemy planes in service?

[At the beginning of 1915 the Farmans seemed to be adaptable to war conditions; they climbed high, they flew fast enough, they were easy to fly. It is only since then that we have discovered their weaknesses and their drawbacks; but it would have been necessary when this was realized to change completely the manner in which orders were given, strike at the self interest, shake up the routines, admit a lack of foresight, and this was too much to ask.

[Then, certain worn out and fearful pilots clung to the Farman. (For circling around the field far from the lines and landing quietly it is a good enough plane.) These pilots fear apprenticeship in a new plane; they extol the crate and its obsolete speed indicator; their point of view was accepted despite the opinion of the young, the real combatants who today suffer the consequences of the errors of others.

[The officers of the technical service, coming from aviation at the start of hostilities or even during peace time, could not admit that their army had changed since their training; they still practiced the ideas of 1912 and refused to move with the times, the times which relegate them to the past.

[Finally, in 1915, at the time of the great modernization of aviation equipment, those at head-

quarters of the army who had had escadrilles at
their disposition gave their opinion on the different types in service. They suspected the Bleriot,
Rep,* Morane for I don't know what reasons; on
the other hand, the chicken coop Maurice Farman seemed to them the ideal observation plane.
It was not at all, but one has to be a combat flier
to know it.

[To be concerned with the tactical application
of aviation was strictly the function of licensed officers.** It is to be regretted that they did not
limit themselves to that but attributed to themselves a technical competence by having taken a
quarter hour flight in an 80 HP Farman in the
1912 maneuvers. It was decreed that "the mono-
plane and the single seater were not adapted to
military use." This view was therefore accepted
and a good number of squadrons of Rep or Bleriot
became Farman or Voisin.***

[These errors *have cost the lives of a great number of
excellent pilots*, young, energetic, and able, who,
knocked down in combat or killed by accidents,
have lost to the aviation arm excellent elements
destined for a bright future. I do not dare to hope
that the errors committed will never receive sanc-
tion or even that they will ever become known.
But when will they give us good machines! When
can we fly without constantly risking a lamentable
accident, fight without feeling invariably at the
mercy of our adversary?

[How much longer will we have these crates?

*Robert Esnault-Pelterie—a good plane. J. B. V.
**Officers from the School of War, more theoretical than
practical. J. B. V.
***Voisin—a rather obsolete plane, withdrawn from service
in 1916. J. B. V.

We have had to fly them for so long that there is little hope of ever seeing them disappear. It has long been discussed by the big shots, but nothing is yet decided. Who will take the initiative in withdrawing them? The builders make the money. The worth of what they deliver to the front means nothing to them. The more machines wrecked, the more they will sell. As to the technical services, they live in the environs of Paris in a pleasant doze, and each evening await the train which will carry them to their homes, put their vigilance to sleep and quiet their misgivings. Besides, their motto is, "Don't worry." We are not the only combatants to suffer from the inferiority of our material. So we have no right to feel specially abused. There is work to do over the lines. But it is sad to think that our ability and our nerve are used not to fight the enemy, but to fight against the poor tools which have been put into our hands.]

Sometimes when the Boche exasperates us and stubbornly tries to interfere with our missions, we lose our coolness and seek to fight any plane no matter how fast it is. But when we have been badly roughed up in a brawl or have seen one of our mates knocked down, we return to our senses, and go back to circling at 3500 feet between the lines and the barrage balloons, while Fritz makes fun of us and comes to taunt us three kilometers over our territory.

. . . June. I am directing artillery fire of a battery of 75's with Basil. We rapidly control its fire on the fortified positions, on junctions of communication trenches, paths on which it will fire in the middle of the night without warning to try to knock out a work, provision, or relief detail. We are bundled in our flight clothes. I have one hand on the throttle, the other on the stick. I twist my neck to find the Boche. Basil, with a cap whose fur comes out at the sides, looks like a young Esquimau. As he is not tall, he stands upright in the cockpit to see better, transmits his messages energetically and from time to time leans toward me to express a profound thought such as: "Things are swell."—"We are having an easy time."—We have them," etc.

Is it a Nieuport or a Boche? . . . a plane descends near us in small spirals and its belly shines as it turns in the sun. "It's a Nieuport," declares the naturally optimistic Basil. "I tell you it's a Boche." It is terribly easy to make a mistake when you see a bus descend in an unfavorable light and when its silhouette is lost in the golden haze of the sun.

It's a Boche. French cannon fire white shell bursts at it. Disgusted, it fires several shots at us and, fearful of having to cross our lines at low altitude, does not dive on us. Basil wants to take up his machine gun to retort. The turret he tries to turn is caught in the wind and pulls him along as it creaks; he fights it, and when the Boche is kilometers away, ends by firing several platonic shots at him. Then he returns to his artillery spotting.

Our battery is always ready. Plenty of others would cease firing as soon as enemy planes appear, lest they should be spotted; this one does not seem to be concerned; it is 6000 feet from the first lines, unsheltered, in full view of the Boches who daily shell it with shells of all calibers.

["Should I say in my report that it would have been well advised to give those guys some of the guns which the division has mobilized to protect headquarters?" asks Basil.]

"Ready," says the battery. "Fire," answers Basil, and we fly straight for our objective to see the four grey and black clouds of the 75 percussion shells hit the target.

Sometimes when we leave the active zone to fly over Talou hill, German cannon fire energetically at us, but the anti-aircraft fire is more impressive than dangerous. Certainly it is irksome, when one promenades in a carcass of wood and canvas, to be pursued for hours by the violent noise of shrapnel, but we know that the hundreds of shots fired daily bring down very few planes, and in practice, the D.C.A.* never prevents us from fulfilling our mission.

"It does not exist," says Basil. "It never did harm to anyone."

Sometimes even, pushed by the demon of perversity, we take pleasure in playing with the bursts which seek us out and miss us, even though the first unexpected shell is always a shock and the bursts which are close shatter our ears and bring a few drops of sweat to the small of the back. But what pilot does not enjoy a little satisfaction in bringing back a few shell fragments in his wings?

As the battery tells us "We don't need you any longer," we observe white shrapnel bursts at 6000 feet over our heads. Four Boches are speeding at 12,000 feet toward Bar-le-Duc. This evening we learn there was a bombardment of the town and for the next two weeks we cannot go to Bar for supplies without receiving rotten eggs and a

*Défense contre aéronefs, i.e., anti-aircraft guns.

rap on the knuckles from the civilians.

We are told that N. . . [Nungesser] knocked down one of the Boches on his return near Saint-Mihiel. May this revenge soften the grocers and winesellers of Bar and let us go buy canned goods, cigarettes and mineral water in their good town without too much risk, where they exploit us with so much enthusiasm.

. . . June. Without consideration for our feelings, they give Basil and me the order to be ready tomorrow morning at daybreak, or at 3:30 a.m. A raid will leave our trenches and we are charged to counter-attack the German cannon during this operation.

A disagreeable awakening. It is cold at 3:00 a.m. in June. The cook, frozen, serves us coffee which is too hot. The hangars are in half light and we nearly stab ourselves on the iron rods of the Bessonneaus with their trickily projecting points. My poorly lighted crate takes on a fantastic appearance and the voice of Octave behind the engine makes me jump. The aforesaid Octave spins my propeller and soliloquizes: "Am I going back to sleep after he takes off!"

I take off without being able to see well and just miss crashing into the trees along the road. Over the lines there is a dense fog. All the vapors of the Meuse separate us from the ground. Impossible to see anything. Artillerymen and infantrymen have to make out for themselves. The enemy planes still in their hangars let us quietly loaf along their lines. We fly over a pearl grey sea. There is not a single French or German crate from the Argonne to Éparges. We are alone. We are cold. We have no function and, without a few holes in the layer which covers the earth, we would be sure to lose our way. Basil, who, to be smart, left this morning in a linen flying suit and no snowboots, is freezing and cannot hold his map. He refuses to admire the sunrise, which, moreover, is dimmed by dark streaks. After an hour and a half of useless patrol, we leave the lines under the general foulness of things and in a sky which becomes thicker and thicker.

It will rain tomorrow.

# IV

. . . June. Mignot, the 2nd lieutenant observer, and sergeant pilot de Sabadil leave this morning at 9:00 o'clock to direct artillery fire of a 75. The ceiling is at 2700 to 3000 feet and we advise them to wait awhile until the sky clears up, but they very rightly say that the work is urgent and they reach the lines.

At ten-thirty a telephone call from headquarters informs us that a craft, range-finding with the artillery division, suddenly dived and crashed in front of our trenches.

Basil leaves immediately with Corporal Larreche to find out what has happened. Indeed he can see the wreckage of a Farman 300 feet in front of the trenches of Rabastens, between the two lines; no question it is the plane of our two comrades. Naturally, there is no one around the debris.

That evening some information filters in to us:

Final Encounter—No Man's Land

the Farman made several passes over the lines at about 3000 feet, heavily shelled by the enemy. Hit by a shot from the ground, the pilot must have slumped over his controls and the plane nose dived into the ground. The infantrymen claim to have seen the passenger throw out papers and maps during the dive. Mignot thus had time to see himself die.

. . . June. During the night an infantry patrol was able to reach the plane. The wings were broken, the fuselage flattened, the motor deeply imbedded in the ground. Nothing of the aviators was found. The Germans beat us to it and took away our dead.

All morning the enemy artillery fired on the debris of Mignot and de Sabadil's aircraft, which caught fire; nothing is left of it.


. . . June. Now what is all this! It is not the usual rumble of barrage firing. This is intense cannonading, serious preparation, punctuated by deafening explosions of large caliber shells. It has already lasted three hours. Have we returned to the very worst days?

"Planes from the squadron are flying, it is no use going up," says the captain, who sees us getting into our flying suits. But we are insistent and we take off to reach the lines.

From the Meuse to the region of Vaux the bombardment causes a great cloud of dust and smoke. One could imagine himself in a sand storm.

What an existence for those who are down there under all that!

A strip of land ten kilometers long and three

deep is being punished relentlessly: even in the air the noise is deafening. The French batteries under attack respond energetically and attempt to counter attack the innumerable German batteries.

Max directs the firing; he takes bearing on thirty new emplacements where German cannon are in action.

We land at 8:00 o'clock. The bombardment does not let up. In the growing dusk the earth seems to crackle and is illuminated by thousands of shell flashes.

At Vadelaincourt everyone is nervous: those who return and have seen, those who, without news, have waited on the ground.

Now what is all this?


. . . June. The Boches attack more strongly than ever. From Douaumont they attempt to descend by the woods on Froideterre and Souville. Once master of these forts, they will dominate Verdun, which will be within arm's reach. It is said our troops have made a serious withdrawal, that Souville is taken, that Fleury is taken. The blackest rumors circulate.

At noon, Carrier leaves with Corporal Segardin to try to unravel our divisional front. At one o'clock a heavy battery telephones us that two aviators of the F.00 have somersaulted near their position, to the west of Verdun, that one of them is seriously wounded in the crash.

We feel a wave of discouragement. There is a jinx on our squadron. These two just after the others. . . . We jump into a car, the captain, Delame and I, and we race to the field hospital which the artillerymen point out to us. Carrier is not badly wounded, he has a broken shoulder blade, a cut face and a very stiff back.

The crate broke up after having turned over in a shell hole. Carrier was thrown out of the cockpit and lost consciousness from the shock. Now he becomes restless and begins to talk. We stop his babbling and leave him to rest. We interrogate Segardin, who escaped with nothing more than a bashed nose and disturbed emotions.

The pilot tells us that, flying at eight or nine hundred feet, they threw out some flares which were not answered; the infantrymen, worn out by a night of fighting, frozen and soaked by the morning downpour, had nothing more with which to signal. And then, one can understand that people who have been shelled for hours and who are enjoying an instant of respite hesitate to reveal their line, in fear of being rained on anew by projectiles.

The ground has been so thoroughly plowed up, the trenches so completely effaced that Carrier could no longer orient himself on this terrain with which he was, however, familiar. The smoke from the explosions trailed between the jagged tree trunks. He saw the dust of grenade battles, but could not distinguish the line itself. It was impossible to see the infantrymen who, covered with mud, blended with the ground.

After fifteen or twenty minutes of useless searching while invisible machine guns shot at them continuously, Segardin heard a bullet hit his propeller, whose tip was broken; the motor started to vibrate terribly, but it still carried our comrades to the south of the Meuse on a narrow terrain where they flipped over in the shell holes.

As we returned to Vadelaincourt, Sessel, who

had taken the place of Carrier over the lines, landed with some information; the Germans should be on the northern edge of Fleury, or seven or eight kilometers from Verdun.

Thus, this front which seemed to be quieting down, has awakened. Again the Boches push with all their strength towards the town; Verdun is more than ever menaced. What is going to happen next?

. . . July. The Germans are already advancing their batteries of 77's on the terrain conquered these last days. We have to go photograph the new emplacements. As de Montault's plane is being repaired, I am given this task.

It is noon, so perhaps we can cross the lines without meeting any Boche barrage. At 6500 feet, not a suspicious silhouette, we speed toward the objective and Max has already started to take his photos when we hear the first shells.

At first two explosions, very low, then above us two ragged black bursts which make us duck our heads in the cockpit; a large greenish 105 so close to us that we pass through its smoke. Another makes my pedals jump under my feet. Max recoils slightly: "I must have photographed the shell instead of the ground," says he smiling. He again leans over the side, much at ease makes his exposure, and then changes his plate without hurrying, in order to avoid scratching it. As for me, I am a bit impatient, I squirm in my seat. It is uncomfortable thus to be among shell bursts, to wait for the possible arrival of a Boche who will catch us redhanded vagabonding over his lines. The photographing takes an eternity and always around us are these angry bursts which seek us out and hem us in. Max has taken ten plates and signals to me to return.

"Look at the dirty dog!"

A plane climbs toward us; he is at 3000 feet lower, but is rapidly gaining elevation; he climbs while turning and each time he tilts, the sun shines on his wing as on a mirror.

"Nothing to worry about—we will be back before he can get us."

Indeed, we are right above the lines when the Boche is 1200 feet below us still in pursuit. It is a Fokker; he must have heard the shell bursts, dropped his lunch and left, tempted by the pretty game which we are. We see him very clearly; he is brand new, his cowling shines, his wings are a straw yellow with the cross of Malta; the pilot seen in horizontal projection, seems to be a rower in his seat.

Max leans over to take a last photo. "He is the one who is taken! I have the portrait of the Fritz!"

I pour on full throttle, and dumping the Fokker, I speed toward the field.

The barrage balloons; no more cannon, no more Boches, not a breath of air, not a cloud, the lovely limpid air where one quietly glides along, the voluptuousness of flying. I cut the throttle and descend very gently.—Who can make us think that aside from the chances of war, aviation can be dangerous?


. . . July. "There he is!" shout the bystanders, raising their arms to the sky. La Fresnaye lands with Delame, rolls an instant; the tail of the crate lifts up, something cracks. The Farman has flipped over and lies on its back.

From all sides the spectators rush to the plane. But the pilot and the observer have been thrown forward out of their seats and already get up, unhurt, feeling their ribs.

The cockpit, made of a ridiculously light plywood, is completely crushed, the gun turret is twisted, the tail spars bent, the wings broken and their skeleton of white pine wood pushes out from the torn canvas. Everywhere are pieces of wire, a tangle of wire. It is for a very good reason that our crate is named chicken coop.

"Tough luck for the crate," says the chief, "or rather, so much the better; it was hexed. Worse would have happened to that lousy machine. It had to have its motor changed three times in two weeks, to say nothing of a wing and a landing gear and at every sortie it brought back all the shell bursts of the sector with it."

Supporting our comrades, a bit dazed and bruised, we go back to the mess.

### Advice

Renaud, by way of an ode, wrote the following commandments *ad usum cage a poulistorum**:

*"If your natural imprudence, the toughness of your chiefs or a contrary fate has won you the dangerous honor of piloting a chicken coop, know at least what you are exposed to, and [also follow this advice in order not to disappear on your first flight and to enjoy for a while longer the light of day.]*

*For the use of chicken coops—a nickname for the Farman planes.

[62]

"Have above all an Etévé,* a good Etévé, well-adjusted which will be your Achates and your Euryale, your confidant and your friend. Even have two of them, one on each side of the cockpit, and don't take your eyes off their florid faces in leaving or in landing, in turning or in straight flight, also during combat [for the boche is less dangerous than your own crate.]

"Be careful when you land: take care not to flip over; the earth is in front of you, your motor is behind: taken between the one and the other you will be compressed and they will have to pick you up with a sponge.

"When you fly be sure not to let the trifles you carry with you slip into the propeller—gloves, glasses, love letters, the antenna—for all such strange bodies will shatter it. In shattering, it will cut the longeron and your stabilizer will separate from the wing. Then you will be obliged to descend in free fall with the whole thing.

"Especially, no acrobatics, n'est-pas! Even the most innocent: let take offs and landings be gentle, departure in a straight line, banking not more than at 35°. I am not speaking of a wing over or a tail spin, and why not loops? [Recall that he who starts to stunt in the crate is preparing a place for himself in the cemetery of Vadelaincourt, so crammed, however, that it already extends as far as Souhesmes.]

"Fly slowly? You're crazy. Full speed, even, or else a side-slip or a tail spin threatens you; with either of them, one does not come out alive.

"Dive? What are you doing there, stupid! Your fragile crate will break up in the air, your wings will fall off. Come down you must! You will reach the ground with only your motor.

"Combats. You have to fight; without that how will you

*Trade name for an air speed indicator, named for its inventor Captain Etévé. J. B. V.

*fulfill your missions, for there are always boches over the lines.*

*"And yet, think, yes think, that in fighting you will be shot down; the machine gun is there as a formality. Resign yourself then, pacific aircraft to which the duel is forbidden, to circle eternally around a barrage balloon.*

*"And then, none of that is of importance. Shot down by the boche or smashed up by your crate, you will always end up by being rubbed out; and of what importance to the duck is the sauce used to eat it?"*

"A bad joke," says the chief.

"No, Captain, a lack of wit, if you find that my story is not funny, but not lack of spirit, because we fly each time we are told to, even more often, and no one has ever balked, no matter what it was, but [we will at least be allowed to say all the truth if we are sacrificed; we are not dupes and we know what we are talking about on the subject of the crates in which we fly."]

. . . July. I have brought a brand new machine from Bar, a pretty F.40, 130 H.P., which my mechanics have worked over. They have put in a transmitter, have refitted the turret and tuned the motor.

"Captain, may I go with Delame to see what the ceiling is of my new crate?"

Delame is always ready; he takes up a camera, a Lewis lighter than a Colt, dresses as if he were going to the pole and climbs in in front of me.

The two mechanics spin the propeller, put the chucks under the wheels and hang on to the edges of the wings while I try out the motor. At full throttle, my motor purrs beautifully; the wind from the propeller stirs up a cloud of dust, causes the spectators to flee, and shakes the canvas of the neighboring Bessonneaus.

"Let go!" I take off; the 130 H.P. rumbles regularly. My passenger sits facing me; we chat while we climb.

At 6000 feet a great layer of cloud comes from the west and turns the horizon grey. The sun hits its edge and makes it shine; its whiteness is as pure as the snow of a glacier; we would like to land on its level field, to sit with our legs hanging over the edge of this paradisiacal balcony.

We climb; twenty-five minutes after take off we are almost at 9000. The air becomes cold, and gets to our necks through poorly closed collars, it chills our teeth when we open our mouths to breathe. The crate climbs more slowly in the rarefied atmosphere; the motor continues to turn without sputtering, but weakens a bit.

10,500 . . . 12,000.*

I have never climbed so high. It is a powerful and new impression. The air is too thin, we yawn in order to breathe, like fish out of water; we have difficulty in moving, in talking; we are on edge, the altitude makes us irritable. It is very cold. The view is incomparable; blocked to the west by the advancing sea of cloud, it extends to the east and to the south very far toward a horizon, not straight, but drowned in a milk-like haze. We see Verdun, Éparges, and the trenches of Calonne, Troyon, Saint Mihiel, Bar and the hangars of

---

*In 1916 few planes of this type could reach 12,000 feet. In 1917 the Spad reached 21,000 feet, but we had no oxygen masks so there was danger of fainting at such heights. J. B. V.

Béhonnes. The solitude oppresses us. The earth is infinitely far; distant also are the small white clouds "in lamb's tails" 6000 feet over our heads. Around us the insubstantial air, nothing distinct, nothing really colored, nothing really solid except our large plane.

12,500.

I beat my hands rhythmically on my knees to thaw out my fingers. The Farman scarcely climbs any higher; it has reached its ceiling. Little by little, the barrier of clouds advances and is about to reach the Meuse; we only have time to descend if we do not want to be caught above its grey immensity.

I cut the throttle and get ready to descend. Delame, leaning over the side, takes a photo which contains on a 13 × 18 plate the forts of Vaux, Douaumont, Froideterre and Souville.

"Look out! A crate over there! Boche or French?"

Impossible to distinguish its nationality. He is coming straight at us. Is he going to attack us? Are we going to have to fight here, so far from everything, without support or help? How alone we are, far from the security of the ground, abandoned, lost!

I dive while turning; Delame, with his numbed hands, takes hold of his machine gun and fights with the drums.

The plane is above us. I twist as I have never twisted, my plane descends at an extraordinary speed in an atmosphere which will not carry it. The earth takes on bizarre positions. Delame, on his knees in his turret, tries to line up the alarming crate in his sights. But the unknown flier does not insist and makes off again toward the north.

Boche or French? Perhaps French wanting to identify us; perhaps a very young Boche who does not know where he is and who lost his nerve at the moment of attacking us. We will never know.

But now the sea of cloud below us has closed in. How are we going to return? We have to fly by compass if we do not want to land among the Boches. Anyone who has not been in an airplane does not know what it is to be lost. The wind, whose direction is unknown, pushes the plane off course. In the lack of instruments, the sun is a deceptive helper. As for the compass, because of the metal in the plane, the magnetos of the motor and of the wireless, it is completely unsteady.

Where are we going to land, without any reference points? We will have to descend blindly into the cotton wad, and if the clouds reach the ground we will crack up before having seen the earth. Are we over our lines, or the Germans'? I drop straight toward what seems to me to be the southwest. The uniformity of the grey froth seems to take away all sense of direction and distance. Forty-five hundred eternal feet and I dive into the opaque cloud. It envelopes us; we cannot see thirty feet ahead of us, even the wings are stumps, our glasses and the instrument panel are covered with mist. We do not know if we are flying horizontally or not, if we are turning or if we are flying straight. This for several minutes and suddenly we see the ground 3000 feet below us.

Vague trenches, a forest. We must be in the Argonne.

"Saint-Mihiel!" shouts Delame; he shows me

the Meuse and the shattered barracks of Chauvon-court.

Thus I made an error of over fifty kilometers; a few more minutes and we would have landed among the enemy.

Flying along the Meuse, we reach Verdun, then Vadelaincourt, and after the cold of altitude, the warmth which circulates our blood again in our frozen fingers makes us suffer like martyrs and almost makes us want to cry out.

# V

"How is the weather, Max?"

"Dirty."

With great pleasure I pull my blanket over my head and sleep a bit more of the good morning sleep.

The freedom to do nothing, a cigarette, hot coffee, the novel put aside for three weeks, guilt-less laziness rocked by the noise of the rain on the tar paper of the roof. What a time for a pilot!

The chief comes into our room in pajamas; seated on the foot of my bed, he makes big talk about the preceding evening; it was tumultuous. Last night the meteorology called us: a heavy storm was predicted—strong wind and probable squalls about twenty-three hours.

At midnight the probable squall was altogether certain. A slashing rain fell, the wind whined and the Bessonneaus, getting some ideas of shaking themselves free, swayed and threatened to flip over like pancakes, wrecking the crates within their shelter. Flying and ground personnel, fraternally united, had to keep a tight hold on the ropes to prevent disasters. The rain, the cold and the inadequacy of our clothing made this little party rather disagreeable, but in contrast how wonderful is this morning of laziness!

Let us enjoy our quiet. Enjoy it, in face of the multiple worries which the afternoon promises. We have to go on a liaison mission by flooded routes frequented by miserable foot soldiers covered with mud. The field will be invaded by people eager for information; streams of artillerymen or infantrymen, grenadiers or student company commanders who have come to "visit the aviation." And every minute will be shaken by the ringing of the exasperating telephone which will ask us this, that or the other, without a minute of respite.

I know that the telephone has turned the conditions of war topsy turvey in shrinking distance, but on the other hand, what a nuisance! It gives birth to two evils: gossip and the absence of the chief.

"Urgent! Send me how many No. 58 helmets your unit possesses."

"My unit has no helmets!"

"Well send me a zero number, on regulation forms, in three copies."

And so it goes, including at night. Without speaking of the thousand and one accounts of operations we have to dispatch, at a given time, in every direction, even if rains have made all activity impossible for several weeks.

But there are graver consequences.

The officers are far from their troops, or rather

"away from them." At the end of the line they are ignorant of their physical and moral condition and feeling and suffering.

The officers don't make sure personally that their orders are carried out.

The personal ascendency, the physical authority of the individuals really made to command become a dead letter, because the subordinates do not *see* their officers.

Neither do the officers see their subordinates; they have no way of knowing the spirit in which an order is received, and thus no idea of the manner in which it will be carried out.

Four reasons which are enough for me to hate the telephone.

While taking it easy, we get dressed, we shave off three days' beard, we fiddle with our toilet a long time neglected, then covered with a rain coat and our feet in snow boots, we confront the rain and the redoubtable mud of the field to make a tour of the hangars.

The old habit of a cavalryman who likes to look over his horse in the stable; we go to see our crates whose ridiculously large wing span encumbers the Bessonneaus of sixty by ninety feet.

"It is going to rain for another day, Lieutenant; I have dropped down your engine, your valves were sluggish," says Octave.

If my valves were sluggish, there is nothing to say. I leave my two devoted mechanics to their task of cleaning the spark plugs, adjusting the ignition and balancing the propeller. I return to write letters, neglected for several weeks.

We have passed a month of disorder in a tent, but now our Adrian hut is finished and we are installed. In common with Max I possess a room of fifty-four square feet. We have two beds, a wooden stool, two shelves for our shoes, a couple of nails for our uniforms, a writing table.

The captain, who has similar quarters, but only for him, at this instant is busy decorating his walls with direction maps. My dog sleeps and barks in his dreams. I write. Max is waiting for me to give him the table. For a long time he has scorned me and kidded my mania of putting black on white, but since a certain leave from which he returned with his emotions in a whirl he challenges me for the ink well and blackens numberless pages which carry his thoughts to Mlle. X. . . , at Nantes (Loire Inférieure).

During the afternoon waves of strangers arrive dripping with rain. They are brought into the Bessonneaus; they are agape before an F.40 and the training lecture begins: "That is the motor; —that, the propeller; —that, the wings, —that the machine gun turret."

"What, you have a machine gun! Then you are a combat aircraft, a pursuit plane?"

We are like the bourgeois who carries a Browning in his pocket; it makes him feel good, but that does not keep him from being cooled off by the apaches.

"Could we see the pursuit planes, the Nieuports, my friend?"

"By all means!"

They want to see the single-seaters which we would like to fly ourselves; deep within, every pilot of a Mefeu,* feels glum at not having a machine which is solid, fast and well-armed.

*Mefeu, i.e., a Maurice-Farman, often disparagingly called a chicken coop.

But when the ox is harnessed to the plow . . .

The chief takes us on distant liaisons: The Army Corps, divisions, heavy artillery and field artillery. We have to agree with all these big shots on what methods to employ, to give an account of the work accomplished and to prepare for future work.

Today it is Peyrussac and I who follow the chief through offices and corridors of these places. And says Peyrussac: "Look, and be quiet old friend.—Look at these big shots, for a dog has the right to look at the bishop, but be quiet, for he hasn't the right to express his opinion."

And the human comedy begins.

We witness [terrible disputes between elements which should work in liaison, help each other, inform each other, treat each other courteously and understand each other.]

For example, not a single regulation clearly fixes the authority of the Bureau of Intelligence of the Army Corps and that of the squadron. The Captain, chief of the Intelligence (information on the enemy), cannot forgive the chief of the squadron for passing directly to the general, information (new trenches, activity of the batteries, arrival of trains in the stations, etc.) which his planes have gathered. It seems to him iniquitous that someone other than himself should approach and inform the big boss.

In the same way, the heart of the squadron chief bleeds when Captain Mathieu speaks of aerial photos before the officers of the Army Corps, and he has done everything to avoid loaning Intelligence his projector and his negatives, fearing that his rival will call attention to himself and look important in setting up the projector and showing the pictures to the student company officers or the apprentice sappers and the new communication officers of the sector.

[In the Office of Operations four or five captains drowse under a lamp and cut out pin ups from "La Vie Parisienne" while only the chief, an intelligent major, but tired, works and thinks. They will awaken and do their best to get hold of the photos and drawings intended for the Chief of Headquarters and which they would like to exploit first.

[Among the artillerymen, more conflicts, envenomed by the fact that our observers being artillerymen and very often young, their old chiefs suffer cruelly in not being able to control them.]

As for the S.T.C.A. (Topographic Section of the Army Corps), it is not a hostile zone, it is an untenable terrain for aviators. A maker of circulars in a good humored mood advises the officer there to work "closely in collaboration and side by side with the Army Corps squadron," but omits to define the limits of his functions and those of our draughting office; from this results a furious stamping around in each other's flower beds. The squadron publishes a map of the sector, duplicated in black. The S.T.C.A. at once elaborates a similar map in dark brown and black in response to which a multi-colored one is immediately made, a rich model, where an F.00 is displayed and catches the view like a poster of patent medicines or baby food.

Finally, the captive balloon, which a humorist has called "the poor relative of aviation," range finds for batteries, observes and spots just as we do. Our work should be completed by that of the balloon; our observations should check each other; however, there is a chasm between us; is the captive independent? Is it under our orders? Nothing says so. The authorities conflict, and susceptibilities are ruffled. They are jealous of us and we despise them, as that must obviously take place between people where one flies about freely in the air while the other remains attached to the end of a string.

Somber, humiliated, turned in upon itself, the soul of a balloonman broods on misfortune.

The major difficulty for aviators is to have to argue and jostle with people who are both their elders and their superiors.

For our chiefs are young, thank God! Captains of thirty, squadron leaders, find themselves in contact with colonels of fifty who are chiefs of staff, little used to the resistance of subordinates who wear only three stripes. As for our aviation chiefs, they are thirty-five years of age and only the G.H.Q. are over them.

How to remedy this? Make our ranks older, or rejuvenate those of other branches. The first solution, which is foolish, would have more chance of success than the second, which is not realisable; the latter would imply such advancement for certain elite individuals that the majority would immediately take umbrage. The ideas of equality deeply imbedded among those who claim to be the least attached to an equalitarian regime, impose in the army rule by elders, ad aeternum.

At the hospital I knew a very intelligent middle-aged captain, a product of the Staff College, on whom they operated for appendicitis. He called loudly, and with good reason, for young chiefs, colonels of thirty and generals of thirty-five, chosen for promotion in defiance of seniority, mother of all our misfortunes.

But despite this opinion he almost died of unhappy indignation on learning that one of his comrades a year younger than he had just been made a major before him.

We rush around the offices of headquarters, trying with varying success to have our methods adopted by people who think they know better than we do how to use [aviation but who know absolutely nothing about it. In their hands it always gives me the impression of a razor left for a child to play with.]

The chief excels in this struggle. We need chiefs who, like him, have character, know how to defend us, do not allow their personnel and materiel to be wrecked at the whim of the first well-groomed puppy who comes by. It is a pluck which should be admired almost as much as that shown in going over the lines. When good pilots are killed or wounded, good crates wrecked, who will remain to do the work, and Lord knows that the effective strength of an escadrille melts rapidly away when it is made to yield to such nonsense.

Ours is a young and brilliant branch. Any reference to it adorns a report. To have something to put under the heading "Aviation" is the secret desire of all headquarters. The practical utility of the operation reported is little important, and little important is the cost of the paragraph.

"Do you know," says Peyrussac, "what should decorate the entrance to the Temple? It is not the classic and banal association of a lantern or of a pennant, but two antique groups which would be much more apt.

"On one side two pugilists in the act of fighting, carrying a pencil behind the ear and on the biceps an arm band decorated with shafts of lightning.* This group would be called 'The Conflict of Powers.' On the other side, the monumental effigy of Mars peddling baloney. This last emblem would show that in these offices the only work undertaken is to 'dispense information.' It would watch over the activity of Onotos,** the Remingtons and the copy presses, as well as over the effort of these young fellows presenting the appearance of military men, who call on the epic Muse to draw up in appropriate language the recital of the exploits of others. [They have reached this wretched notion of the superiority of the spectacular operation over the useful one. So that in order to have something striking to put on record, to give a show of activity for an outfit that has done nothing, to save an officer from reproach of weakness or inaction, one will use trickery, stretch the truth, and end by making a test flight, a sortie over the lines, and the single shot of a look-out appear to be a repulsed attack.]

"Those who know how to bring in a finished communiqué please the command more than the workers who give straight information, the unvarnished recital of what they have done and what they have seen. [Look at these appointed tailors of truth. Here they bestow a charming cloak on it when it is disgraceful. Here, following the mode, a dress is shortened or lengthened or taken in. They add frills to it, flounces and lace. It is here that bluff is organized. Be content when it is not based on an expenditure of costly material, money and human lives.]"

*Staff officers wore an arm-band with lightning bolts as a symbol. J. B. V.
**A make of typewriter, long discontinued. J. B. V.

# VI

It is a habit as old as aviation. After we have flown for three weeks, when "we are fed up," we are like the frogs who wanted a king and we clamor for rain. But after a couple of days' wet spell, we are bored, we do not know what to do, we walk around our planes, and loudly demand good weather.

You will not understand that, you who creep on the ground; when one loves aviation, one loves it, and that's all. One loves it like a mistress, and even if a bitch, a whore, a poison, even if, like a female spider, it devours its lovers, I recommend it to you, for I find it irresistible.

Leaving this morning, after days of mist, I am full of bright joy. Wedged into the bottom of my seat, I am light-hearted in piloting my crate which climbs in the calm air. I am happy. Those who fly a plane more maneuverable and faster than my crate can kid me; so what! I go very high and very fast,—I fly just as they do.

It is impossible to express what piloting is, it cannot be talked or sung about. One is or is not one of the fraternity. As for me, I know that if one day I am injured and incapable of flying, if after the war, I do not have a crate at my disposal, I could never look at a pure sky, nor see a plane fly over, without being heartsick with regret for my wonderful hours as a pilot.

All the machines of the sector, German and French, have left their hangars after the days of forced inaction. On each side we spot artillery, we cross paths, we observe.

As the forces are about equal, it is truly like a trench in the air; each stays in its position, watches

and waits. Bad luck for a lone flyer who passes
into the opposed zone. He is immediately surrounded by a swarm of enemies who attack him
and usually knock him down.

All of these planes, separated only by an
imaginary barrier—for after all, the lines do not
extend into the sky—have the inexplicable look
of fish in an aquarium divided by an invisible
glass.

. . . August. Basil and Renaud left quite early
this morning to spot artillery; it is nine o'clock
and we see them land, taxi on the field, and stop
in front of us. Renaud, excited, loosens his belt,
rises from his seat, pulls off his glasses and shouts:

"We knocked one down!"

Basil, calmer, hands us his map, gets out of the
plane, takes off his helmet and says:

"We knocked one down easily and completely."

"A what?"

"A Boche."

"What do you mean, a Boche?"

"Yes, we got one; knocked him down, knocked
him down!"

Basil explains:

"We had climbed to 12,000 during our artillery
spotting not to be bothered by the Boches nor by
the anti-aircraft. We saw a big crate which climbed
toward us, a two-seater, which was pushing as
hard as it could. It took quite a while to arrive.
When it was 600 feet away I started to fire. It was
knocked down at the 100th round! It began to fall
waveringly like a dead leaf, sliding from time to
time on one wing and the other. It must have had
a control cut or the pilot knocked about so he did
not know what he was doing. What is sure is that
the machine fell from 12,000 feet straight to the

ground and now rests on its back or on its wheels (I don't know which) three kilometers from the first line between two trenches."

"No kidding?"

"No kidding, you can go take a look."

"I'm going to do better than take a look," said Montault, "I'm going to go photograph your Boche; with that no one can challenge you."

And he takes off with Delame armed with a camera.

We have seen the photo, the Boche sprawled in the middle of it incontestably, unanswerably; then Max and I left to direct 75 fire on it, and after several shots it burned.

The authorities confirmed a German plane knocked down by Basil and Renaud in a Farman 130 H.P.*

It is in this way from time to time that a Farman demolishes an enemy aircraft which is jinxed or clumsy. It is our revenge, inoffensive martyrs, to strike back once in awhile at those who rub us the wrong way. It is a very rare revenge, for these victories are few [when compared to the innumerable Farmans knocked down.]

This evening the phonograph is playing in honor of Basil and Renaud, overcome with their luck and who have not yet recovered from their sudden change of role—that of official victims to that more agreeable one, accidentally, of hunters.

---

*The incident here related did not befall the fliers designated under the names Basil and Renaud but happened to my observer Cyril Lebarbu (later killed) and to me. J. B. V.

## VII

"And you won't forget our letters?"

"It's a promise," answers de Montault.

How could he forget? They make a package big enough to burst his pockets.

Astride Pierre's shoulders, he reaches the car which will take him to the train; this style of transportation will prevent muddying the new boots destined to fascinate his lady pen pals, for Montault is going on leave.

"Go get a rest," says the captain; "you have done enough for the last three months, you have a right to your week off."

To which Renaud adds: "Man is made for war and woman for a warrior's rest; but try not to rest up to the point where you will be totally useless when you return from Paris."

And Montault is gone.

The most obvious thing about this event is that I find myself a photographer for a week. I am delighted; for the daily routine of artillery spotting was weighing heavily on me. It is the job of a squirrel in a cage.

Artillery spotting—that means to remain for hours in the air serving a battery which has no concern for you and which has fired twenty cannon shots when you land because of lack of gas. It is eternal circling like a goat tied to a stick, between a transmitter and an objective. It is to pilot a mediocre and tiresome machine. It is to offer your back to shells and to attacks of enemy planes, without hope of returning the blows.

We spot, we spot ceaselessly all kinds of guns.

We must even find the range for the trench mortars, but the waywardness and inaccuracy of these guns, their enormous and unexpected dispersion have caused this effort to fail. There remain the cannons, all the cannons, small, large, rapid fire, slow fire, long and short; 75's, the 90's, the 95's, the naval 100's, the 120 longs, the 155 Schneiders; the junior 65 like the grandfather 220 is our client, without speaking of a Russian cannon which came to Verdun I don't know how, is used by I don't know whom, is the only one of its kind, and finally has no name, for its bizarre caliber can only be expressed in the measurements of its nation.

Now, while we carry on a radio dialog with the artillery, Montault is covering himself with glory in photographing all that is photographable in the sector—the lines, batteries, ammunition dumps, shelters, communication trenches, the big gun which used to fire on Dugny, trails, billets, balloons with their windlass, a little Decauville* with its plume of smoke and even the Adrian hut of the general of the Army Corps, with its little garden kept up by the secretaries and the number of the Army Corps outlined with shell cases in a flowerbed in the form of a heart.

All of these photos (except those whose aim is purely artistic) are of great help to artillery and infantry headquarters; they give minute information on the works of the enemy, on the configuration of the terrain, on the exact emplacement of our troops. They also serve to correct the maps

*A narrow-gauge portable railway which can readily be taken up and relaid in any desired location. Named for its deviser Paul Decauville (1846-1922), a French industrialist.

and to establish detailed maps for the artillery.

Montault gives himself entirely to his work. He thinks, he dreams only of his photos. All day long, with raised eyes, he waits for a brief opening in the sky. He leaves in the middle of a meal, at dawn or the last moments before dusk. He has learned this primary truth that, from the ground, no one can know if the visibility in the air will be good or bad. Therefore, he goes up two or three times a day to check and ends by finding the right time.

Moreover, his passion is disinterested. In flying this way among the Boches, in a chicken coop, generally without protection, he clearly runs the risk of being shot down. His fellows esteem and honor him, but the people to whom his photos come cannot appreciate the courage and skill they represent. Try to make a desk man who, between his telephone and his master map, leafs the proofs, understand the trouble taken to obtain them. For him, everything, the chauffeur who drives a truck, an infantryman who leaves the trench, a pilot in his cockpit, all are reduced to diagrams. A diagram is never frightful nor admirable.

I remember urgent photos which a division clamoured for over the telephone and which de Montault took in really dirty weather at 2500 feet and far into Boche lines.

The chief at headquarters who received them looked at them without enthusiasm; he was about to put them on a pile of old papers when his face lit up. He had just discovered one where the outline of the trenches vaguely caricatured a profile.

"Look! A cartoon," said he.

That is all we could get from him in blame or praise.

What Montault brings back from the lines, Delame, head of the photographic section, develops and makes the most of with special personnel in a hut reserved for his use alone.

Several reservists, professional photographers, develop the plates and make the proofs, load the cameras and repair them. These are likable, hardworking and devoted people. At times a great effort is asked of them. Sometimes in a single day, forty exposures 18 x 24 are brought to them of which fifty or sixty copies each must be printed urgently, in all, 2000 copies. The crew spends the entire afternoon and night at work, which is rough going despite coffee, the quarter liter of wine and the cold supper which are allowed for the occasion.

Two thousand proofs of extreme urgency! Where are they going, ye gods? Distributed abundantly in headquarters of the army, the Army Corps, the division and the brigade, they rarely get as far as the command posts of battalion chiefs; never to the troops. The captains and the section chiefs at times receive some in the command post of their major, but they cannot carry them away to use them in place; they have no other recourse than to make an unclear and imprecise sketch.

It is a pity, for if these photos are indispensable to the big shots who command the large units, they cannot be less so to those who should be able to study, shell hole by shell hole, the terrain they will have to cross at the moment of assault.

Now, seeing the number of copies which we make, each section chief could have the photo of his little sector, no more than two weeks old, without affecting the number of copies sent to the superior echelons. But this is an impossible ideal to realize. The intermediaries cause these photos destined for the troops to disappear, keeping them in their archives or consecrating them to mere red tape, [of which the use, entirely theoretical, is only felt by its authors. There must also be collections! The girl who sends packages* to the interpreter or the little cousins of the captain of the gendarmerie in charge of carrying the mail and the sister of the second lieutenant of hussars commanding the escort, doubtless arrange in their albums these photos which we have sought in the midst of bullets and anti-aircraft shells.]

Lieutenants and infantry captains have told us they never have had their own aerial photo. They considered them a rare and precious commodity. A visit to the Delame factory has put them straight; they left with their pockets full of prints. Since then we send the copies directly to the line regiments. But how to explain that we did this without going through channels, and that not one of these memorandums which are sent to us in such numbers orders the distribution of photos to those who have the greatest need.

Speaking of the personnel of the photo section, how can I omit Leclerc, an architect in civil life, draughtsman for F.00 squadron and a monomaniac in his incarnation as warrior. Bent all day long over the prints, the negatives, the positives, a magnifying glass in his hand, he scrutinizes them, he finds what would remain hidden to everyone else. He has engraved in his eye the smallest detail of the sector. He can see, on a photo brought to him

*The French word *marraine* (godmother) was applied in the First World War to a young girl or woman who "adopts" a soldier, sending him packages of food or articles of use.

still wet, that the Boches have made a new lookout slit at the salient of the Zouaves, that two wheelbarrows of fresh dirt have been taken out of sap 43-91 and that the Ludendorff communication trench being flooded, the fatigue parties go by a parallel path in order not to wet their feet.

He has rendered noteworthy service in interpreting with astuteness and perspicacity hundreds of photos; but he has paid for this devotion by a mild madness. He is obsessed by his specialty; he no longer talks of anything except trenches, paths, camouflaged batteries. He no longer knows if it is daylight, if it is raining, if dinner is served. His life is condensed in the microscopic reproduction of this landscape which he has not seen and will never see, because he does not go up in a plane. A conscientious and resigned monomaniac, he admits that his dreams are haunted by the interwoven network of trenches and that while on leave with his wife and his youngsters, he cannot detach his mind from the obsession of the photos at the squadron.

. . . August. A division requests angle shots at low altitude. The pleasure falls to me of executing this kind of mission I know nothing about.

We take off without gaining elevation, skimming the roads where the lines of trucks are bottled up, the villages crammed with troops, the stripped woods full of fox holes. In an instant we are over Verdun.

I had never flown so low over Verdun. At six thousand feet may be seen streets, squares, crossings which still form a town. At six hundred feet can be seen only a skeleton of a city. Every house which is not completely destroyed, has its roof knocked off or has been gutted by shells. Perhaps there is not a single one in Verdun which can be repaired and which must not first of all be levelled before being entirely reconstructed. The center and the west of the town are less damaged, but of the northern quarters and suburbs and the region which borders the Meuse, nothing remains but piles of stones, tiles, slate and debris which still vaguely outline the rectangle of the walls; Verdun is dead, very dead and the mason can only come after the demolition squad.

We fly over the Pavé suburb. A battery of artillerymen are in the orchards and in the gardens. They take shelter in cellars, protected by the debris of the collapsed houses; the hewn stones make a breastwork for their cannon.

Beyond the canal, one enters desolation. On land pocked with shell holes filled with greenish water, hollowed by the labyrinth of trenches of the third line, one does not see a living being. Supplies and reliefs are brought up during the night, and during the day men proceeding alone follow the communication trenches, less dangerous than roads. Even the trees have disappeared, levelled by the bombardment, then burned by the soldiers.

In a small farm house whose broken red roof lays bare the pattern of rafters and beams, protected from the view of German observers, is a group of engineer sappers who wave at us with their caps. I go down low enough to see them, in shirt sleeves, shaving, mending their uniforms or oiling their guns. They salute us for having visited them in the uneasy isolation, the troubled silence, which constitute their existence bowed under the menace of cannon.

Scarcely have we left them than we are over the lines. I did not know, as I had seen it only from a great height, that Froideterre hill was so elevated. Flying low as we were, it dominates us and towers over the French line anchored to the flank of the hill.

As long as we pass in front of the German trenches, the machine guns and cannon send bullets and shells at us, but without any precision, for our unusual altitude throws them off. As we fly over this bizarre fortification in the shape of a crab which all know who have been at Verdun, a 210 explodes on a communication trench a hundred and fifty feet below us, shakes up our Farman and sends several fragments into our wings.

Shrapnel follows us, and bullets clatter. We hang for an instant over this desolation oppressed by a deceitful calm, then we leave, taking two last pictures, one over the fort of Souville, its moats filled, its superstructure eaten away by the bombardment and whose turrets, however, still fire, the other over the flooded banks of the Meuse toward Bras and Vacherauville. We return weaving our way between the cables of the balloons in order not to hit one of them, a foolish accident, which would not be the less mortal.

. . . August. ". . . The whole picture will include the enemy lines up to the light batteries. We will use white gouache for the major communication trenches, red gouache for the German trenches, and green for the French trenches. All of that will make a panel a meter long for the office of the general."

[87]

If it is for the office of the general, there is no hesitation . . .

We take off to be the portrait maker of German battery 87-51 situated in a ravine at six short kilometers behind the German lines and which the said whole picture lacks. The pursuit squadrons, reduced by the damage and the wear and tear of their crates, are not able to furnish me any protection, for they fly only at the time set for their patrols. Thus I leave at the same time as two Farmans of the squadron flown by Max and Carrier, who are going to direct artillery fire over the lines. They are going along with me on my mission and I hope that the Boche planes, kept respectful by a group of three Farmans, will let me take a shot up to their batteries without bothering me.

But I barely get my action underway when a little two-seater bores in on us and in no time at all, fires a burst from his two machine guns. He makes us give way. However, as I need the picture, after consulting with Delame, my passenger, I take advantage of a moment, followed by the faithful Max, when the Boche is at some distance, to go for the objective.

But he is a rapid beast; scarcely have I finished my photo, when he is on me and attacks from so close that I can distinguish the smallest details: his dirty white canvas, the black crosses on his wings, fuselage and rudder, his turret from which his machine gunner fires incendiary shells with long white tails which whine in our ears. He circles around me at will and is never in my angle of fire. Finally, a sharp turn, to line him up and Delame fires a burst of his Colt at him, so severe that, disgusted, he leaves us to attack Max who comes to the rescue.

The Boche approached Max twice, so close that I thought they were going to collide. He attacked him violently, then he returned to attack me. He was really a good pilot, flying a good crate. He glued himself to my rear stabilizer, and much as I maneuvered I could not break away. I don't know how many shots he fired, but the noise from his machine gun deafened me, and, because of his position, Delame could not return the fire. I thought myself shot down, especially when two cables of my aileron broke, either because I dived too steeply or because a bullet cut them.

Carrier, who was high above and could do nothing, threw up his arms it seemed and cried out to his pilot "they have had it!" But it was not for this time. At 4500 feet over the Meuse, the Boche let us go, and we could put on the power and reach our field.

During this time, Max had returned, flying slowly. Fifteen or so bullets had hit around his cockpit, cutting the cables, one entering the fuselage, half severing a longeron. I do not understand how neither he nor his pilot were hit, and how we all got out of it in such good shape.

We land. We get out of the crate. We look at the damage. We are slightly stiff and we cannot help thinking by how small a chance we were able to return to the security of the solid earth instead of being a pile of canvas and wood and other things after a vertical fall from 6000 feet.

... A sharp wit whose spines were not always turned outward, and he often pricked
himself on the spikes of his own criticism . : .
                                    Anatole France

"Peyrussac is our evil genius" says the captain;
"he plays the Cassandra of the escadrille; he
criticizes everything and everyone, and predicts
disasters for France."

In truth our friend cannot prevent himself from
looking at ideas, decisions, orders, institutions in
all their aspects and these are not always pretty.
His acute judgment is unsparing, and he is wrong,
according to some, in airing his mind to those
around him. Moreover, sincere and upright, he
does not spare self criticism.

We tell him, "You destroy institutions which
certainly do not amount to much, but which it's
untimely to destroy. At another time we would
willingly leave them in your clutches, but it's not
quite the right moment to diminish their prestige."

But Peyrussac loves his country and, out of
love, although it hurts him, he exposes its slightest defects, the same way one bitterly finds fault
with the imperfections of the beloved woman one
would wish to be irreproachable.

"How should I not be pained by errors and failures? I have left a good part of myself in the war;
I drag my leg, and my hand no longer closes. I am
thus more concerned in the victory than the
majority of Frenchmen, having sacrificed more for
it. I am going where my money is."

An artillery officer, he was wounded at the
Marne. He joined aviation at the end of 1914; he
took part in the attack on Notre-Dame-de-Lorette,

on Souchez and on Carency as well as in the September offensive in Champagne. He was wounded in January, 1916, by a bullet in the arm in a combat over Tahure, and returned to the F.00 only last May.

Such is the one who plays the role of tireless faultfinder among us. He is equally critical in his judgments of the front and rear.

"I have seen too much at Paris," he says, "not to have . . . . . . . . . . . . . . . . . . . . . . . . . . . . . . .
. . . . . . . . . . . . . . . . . . . . . . . . . . . . . . . . . . . . . . .
. . . . . . . . . . . . . . . . . . . . . . . . . . . . . . . . . . . . . . .
. . . . . . . . . . . . . . . . . . . . . . . . . . . . . . . . . . . . . . .
. . . . . . . . . . . . . . . . . . . . . . . . . . . . . . . . . . . . . . .
. . . . . . . . . . . . . . . . . . . . . . . . . . . . . . . . . . . . . . .
. . . . . . . . . . . . . . . . . . . . . . . . . . . . . . . . . . . . . . .
. . . . . . . . . . . . . . . . . . . . . . . . . . . . . . . . . . . . . . .
. . . . . . . . . . . . . . . . . . . . . . . . . . . . . . . . . . . . . . . "

The rear, the near front—these are places full of allurements and full of baseness and it is this baseness which it is prohibited to reveal. Don't reveal that which should remain in shadow, or else they will make it hot for you. The old myth of Psyche is always true. Certainly, this handsome young man, Cupid, was disturbed by the untimely light, his hand was burned by the boiling oil, but, all considered, it was Psyche who was caught again at the turning point and who was in the soup.

On returning from liaison, my friend tells me: "During the six months of my absence, the army has been shaken up. I had to relearn everything of infantry, artillery and aviation, which have changed their style of fighting, of disposing of their effectives, of organizing their units, and in a word have changed their methods from top to bottom.

But I have found the headquarters of our Army Corps just the way it was.

"They are the same officers as at D. . . in Champagne where I have left them. They are seated in the same order as before, at the same desks, where I imagine they have carved their names. It is true that some have been decorated, but it is the only change that can be observed. They have kept their long hair, the tender rose of their cheeks and the unfaded blue of their uniforms, innocent of rain and mud. [Especially, and this is more serious, they have kept a narrow mind, a sleepy brain, the short view of the bureaucrats who see the troops on a roster of effectives, trenches on a map, combats in a report. Everything stagnates in this office. There, between a typewriter and a telephone, one always imagines himself qualified to lead 30,000 men into fire with the procedures of the army schools, the formulas and theories of manuals which were already old at the Marne and the Yser.]

"Our headquarter officers, with very few exceptions . . . . . . . . . . . . . . . . . . . . . . . . . . . . . . . . . . . .
. . . . . . . . . . . . . . . . . . . . . . . . . . . . . . . . . . . . . . . . .
. . . . . . . . . . . . . . . . . . . . . . . . . . . . . . . . . . . . . . . . .
. . . . . . . . . . . . . . . . . . . . . . . . . . . . . . . . . . . . . . . . .
. . . . . . . . . . . . . . . . . . . . . . . . . . . . . . . . . . . . . . . . .
. . . . . . . . . . . . . . . . . . . . . . . . . . . . . . . . . . . . . . . . .
. . . . . . . . . . . . . . . . . . . . . . . . . . . . . . . . . . . . . . . . .
. . . . . . . . . . . . . . . . . . . . . . and for my part I resign myself with difficulty to work under their orders and to be in constant contact with them.

"I am well aware that an intermediary is needed between the troops and the aviation. We should thus live in good relations with those people, who are the least likely to please us, the least likely to appreciate us. It is a marriage of convenience, in all its horror. A long time ago I was taught there were no perfect marriages, but at most some good ones. In any event ours is detestable, though for all our sins we are undeserving of it."

# IX

. . . 21 August. For several days the sector has been in an extremely agitated state, and the work of artillery spotting is getting heavier. Perrin trench and a part of the trench of Deux-Minen make an enclave in our lines about 1000 feet long by 500 deep. This salient has become the phobia of the Army Headquarters, which is preparing an attack to capture it. In preparation for this operation, all of the available pieces are directing their fire on the trenches to be taken and on the barrage batteries which are attempting to prevent it.

The attack will take place day after tomorrow. Sessel will be in charge of the infantry liaison, and will mark out the new line; other crews will take care of the opposing fire. I intend to fly with Max at the time of the assault as artillery plane.

. . . 22 August. It is abominable weather; the clouds rake the roofs of the Bessonneaus; a fine and uninterrupted rain falls; the weather vane has turned to the west and stays there.

Will we attack tomorrow? The jump off trenches must be flooded, the attack troops frozen and soaked. As for us, if this weather persists, we cannot help either the infantry or the artillery.

. . . 23 August. They telephone us this morning that the attack took place. It is impossible for us to make a sortie; it is no longer raining, but the fog is at ground level. Sessel tries to take off, gets lost in the dense fog and just misses hitting a Bessonneau in landing.

At noon, with still the same weather, we are informed that the objectives have been taken without serious losses and that ground liaison has been established.

. . . 24 August. The earth is still so wet that the clouds condense at a hundred feet in an opaque ceiling. We cannot see the end of the field. Not a single squadron takes out its planes. I take off to try to take Max to the lines, but we risk getting lost. We have only vertical vision. We reach the trenches and only with difficulty find the area of attack. It is impossible to carry on a counter fire with this thick curtain before one. Besides, the sector is calm.

At fourteen hours, a telephone call; the Boches counter attack. For more than an hour they have carried out a violent artillery preparation on our new line which we do not hear because of the direction of the wind. Naturally, all communication is cut. The Army Corps demands that a plane be sent at once to untangle the situation.

Should Sessel leave? The fog is thick, he certainly will not do any good; he will get lost or get shot down by ground fire; after consultation with his pilot Gilbert, he gets dressed, takes his map and his rockets and leaves. "The infantrymen are getting their heads knocked off; it is necessary to go boost their morale, and it will please them to see a plane!"

As we predicted, he did not gather any kind of information; scarcely taken off, he disappeared into the clouds. Over the lines, he was not able to untangle anything, because he was not high enough to distinguish the whole layout of the trenches and to have any reference points. Furthermore, the infantrymen did not have any more signals to make their positions known. He saw only one fire in a vague shell hole, which might have been lit by the Germans. But he flew for half an hour at a hundred feet over our troops, launched twenty rockets, all the sector saw him, all of the German machine guns fired on him. He returned with his plane riddled with bullets and the ceiling was so low that he had to follow the roads not to get lost.

During the night the liaison men arrived at Army Corps. They reported that Perrin Trench and the Trench of Deux-Minen were again lost, that the remainder of the attack battalion were dispersed in shell holes at about the position of the old shove off lines. They added that as the battalion was cut off from liaison, fought with grenades and risked being circled, a Farman, which for half an hour had suffered intense fire, had come to show them that they were not entirely forgotten by the command and lost to the rest of the world. [Perhaps in waiting for a more favorable day to launch the attack, it would have been possible to avert the loss of the conquered trenches. In good weather the troops would not have been demoralized by a night of waiting in the rain.

[The supplying of munitions and of food would have been easier, as well as liaison on foot (after the rains of the preceding days, the ground was a hopeless morass of mud).

[95]

[Finally, the planes would have been able to see the German artillery preparation from the beginning, contribute to check the attack, and direct fire on the batteries, the jump-off trenches of the adversary, and on his reserves.

[. . . August. I don't know if the commander of the Army Corps has resigned himself to accept this blow to his pride, but for the moment the Perrin salient remains in the hands of the Boches. Moreover, the general condition of the morale of the army of Verdun is not favorable to attacks. All attention is turned toward the offensive of the Somme. Here the effectives are reduced on the ground as well as in the air, and the munitions are doled out for the artillery.

[When we have no range finding to do, Max and I are allowed to cruise for an hour or two over the lines to locate batteries in action and if need be to bring down reprisal fire on them. There is work to do, for the ravines of the Cote du Poivre are full of 77's and near nightfall one can see the muzzle flashes of the guns.

[Yesterday, when we were directing the fire of a 155 long toward Vacherauville, a German single-seater attacked a plane of the F . . . which was flying at about 3,000 feet in our lines. The Boche approached without being seen and fired only one burst. At the first bullets the Farman caught fire and fell near Fleury.

[As a matter of fact, we are in a period of bad luck. The same day the captain who commanded Squadron G.4, a neighbor of ours, did not return from a photo reconnaissance. We do not know how he was knocked down. The balloons saw nothing; not a single observer signaled combat.

[. . . September. Max was decorated today. We were all delighted; none among us more merits such an honor than this intelligent, courageous and energetic boy who carries his spirit of duty to a point of austerity.

[There was a general distribution of crosses and of medals to the squadrons of Vadelaincourt, a ceremony during which three Nieuports gave a stunning exhibition. The celebration was more intimate among us; at lunch all of the F.00 drank to its intelligence officer and the captain embraced Max warmly. The boss had worked for a long time to get this cross for his best observer. I have never seen a chief take so much trouble to reward the merits of his subordinates, which is an admirable quality if one adds that he has never uselessly endangered the life of those who are under his orders.]*

. . . September. Today I had to make five or six flights of twenty minutes to give the trainees of the squadron a baptism of air. It means climbing to 3000 feet, going as far as the balloons, giving a distant view of the lines to the passengers, who, moreover, do not distinguish them, for a certain amount of practice is needed to see from the air; finally, returning for a landing on the field, a landing during which, clinging to the edge of the cockpit, the trainees watch the earth come up with eyes starting out of their heads.

I hate this kind of work. Outside of combat missions, I do not like to fly, whether it is, to take up a neophyte or to do a demonstration before some passing big-wig. Accidents lose us almost as

*This passage, though not censored, did not appear in the printed text. It is here added, with the approval of the author.

many people as do combats and shells, and it is too foolish to risk one's life for the curiosity of a stranger or the gratification of his sporting instincts. Now, I by no means think it is seriously worth while to fly around for twenty minutes officers who are sent to us at the F.00.

Orders are very strict in obliging us to have constantly mixed among us, in our squadrons of the Army Corps, the Philistine crowd of these trainees.

Staff officers, artillery communication officers, intelligence, infantry signal officers come by groups of six or seven to spend a week among us, eating and lodging with us, living in the squadron.

Naturally this contact is indispensable for confidence, for mutual understanding and for morale, but what a source of bother! What is there to show these wretched fellows after they have once made a tour of the house? They drag around all day in their inaction and boredom. If we do not take them up, they are annoyed, feeling there is ill will on our part and declaring the training useless. If we take them up, this serves no purpose except to give them a new thrill, a sporting impression at the risk of an accident, and at the price of wearing out the planes. Now, in 1916, we have other fish to fry than to give pleasure of this type to the officers of neighboring arms, when we lack good pilots, when an hour of flight comes to an exorbitant price and the planes which are slowly constructed and which we rapidly wreck, are given to us in dribbles.

The only officers who should have an interest in flying over the sectors are the big shots of the divisions and of the Army Corps. But their importance glues them to their desks. At present a course of instruction for staff officers being anticipated, they have sent us a second lieutenant of dragoons in charge of the grooming of the general's horses. He seems to be a bit dumb and was air sick on his first flight. I do not see how his aerial instruction was at all urgent.

Certainly there are among the trainees brave comrades, without hostility, and without jealousy, but this is far from being the usual case; it is annoying not to be among your own, not to be able to speak freely, to feel the presence of an ill disposed stranger, an incompetent stranger who understands poorly and repeats even more poorly what he has heard. It is terribly nerve wracking not to be able to take a step without getting tangled up with some fidgity person who is always under foot, asks the most useless questions, is determined when it rains to take a hop, a little hop, and will have taken off in a supply truck to go to Bar to see a passing cousin, just on the day his unit telephones to demand his urgent return.

# X

After leaving us like Old Mother Hubbard before her empty cupboard, the army aviation has consented to replace several of our oldest crates: "The sector was asleep, we are told; it is going to wake up and we are going to strengthen the squadrons in materiel and in personnel."

My old war horse, the 1847, is going to delight some school and perish in the hands of a recruit.

Headquarters gives me 2599, just arrived at the annex. Thus I leave for Bar to look for 2599. At Bar, there is no 2599. They can offer me other F.40's; number 2560, 2603, and even 2587 which has had one of its struts bent in landing. But of the machine I am looking for, not a trace!

I return by road to Vadelaincourt and report its absence to the army which, astonished, telephones to the proper authority. The proper authority answers that 2599 has left the depot in Paris and should be at the front and that in any case the rear is no longer responsible. There are sharp interchanges on the telephone. The adjutants tear their hair, until, by a stroke of genius, one of them thinks of telephoning the neighboring army, which tells him that indeed a plane is there, that there was no order for it, and that this phantom crate is at our disposition at Chalons* where we can come and get it.

And thus we alight at Chalons—Peyrussac who will be my passenger on the return, I and finally Octave, carrying the huge bundle of a tool kit, two flying suits, two helmets, an altimeter and an air speed indicator.

Followed by my acolytes I immediately go to the Aeronautical Headquarters to claim my goods. An adjutant receives me, unfriendly, moreover. They cannot give us the 2599. "As it was here for more than a week, it has been appropriated and it no longer belongs to you." I lift my arms to the sky, and exhibit my service order, plead formal promises, the trip, the time lost, the displacement of three people, and finally am able to push the adjutant toward his telephone where he asks for the

*The name was disguised as Z_____ in the French original.

adjutant of our army. Let these lesser functionaries untangle things among themselves!

Quite a lively conversation ensues, we hear: "Urgent need—assignment already decided—special installation anticipated—work almost finished," but when the receiver is violently hung up, we have won our case; we leave carrying a bit of paper which will allow us to take possession of the machine in litigation, and fly to the devil with it.

At the field (four kilometers on foot, for headquarters does not wish to furnish us a car) we are shown the hangar where we will find No. 2599; in the cockpit a greasy mechanic is working, pliers in his hand, his lips clamped over cotter keys; Octave questions him:

"What are you doing to the crate?"

"I am putting in dual controls."

"Why?"

"For someone who wants to learn to fly."

"Who wants to learn on a brand new wagon?"

"Captain X. . . . , tactical adjutant of the army."

"He overdoes things, the mec," says Octave.

There is a good half day's work to undo what has been done and to put the plane back in shape. I leave Octave and we start out, Peyrussac and I, for Chalons where we will eat lunch and hunt for a place to rest.

"He really piles it on, the adjutant. Isn't that right, Perruche?"*

["Yes, but not much more than those adjutants that I have seen during the attacks on _____ having dual controls installed at a time when things were at the worst and forgetting everything that inter-

*Perruche (parrot) was Peyrussac's nickname.

[101]

fered with getting their much-desired license. To get a flying license is an obsession with certain officers. It is the official stamp, the trademark, which will give them entry to the posts that they covet in the numerous services, in the delicious cheese which aviation, our poor aviation, offers them at headquarters or in the rear.

["They are a whole black band come to colonize us. Certified at the War College or not, they join us not to fight, but to make their way. They arrive as observers; that is easiest, the quickest done, does not require *much* apprenticeship. Naturally they do not remain in an escadrille where blows are received and where one moulders in work and obscurity. They slip into some sort of job in a headquarters where they take flying lessons. It is easy enough in an old model Farman and as soon as they have their flying license they go to some safe spot in the rear where the title of pilot (God knows why) is required."]

"Perruche, you are unreasonable; as soon as you leave the troops, your one-sidedness becomes outrageous, and your wrath carries you away at the sight of an officer, from an insignificant lieutenant to the most unpretentious of majors. Spare! I beg you, spare those of our arm; we do not have headquarters in aviation,—or so few that it is not worth talking about them."

"That is true, the local commands are scarcely headquarters; decent fellows are not lacking there who have proven themselves, still fly, pay with their persons and get shot down like good guys; those I esteem and admire, but people are still to be found there that I would like to [see disappear forever—the armchair tacticians, those who have lost their nerve, and the old aviators.

["The tacticians, those are the ones I was talking to you about. They have one great fault: they play a role in aviation, and they are not aviators. One is not an aviator for having flown twenty-five hours over an airdrome, and four or five flights toward the balloons. But they are taken for such by unenlightened strangers; they have our insignia, our slang, our pay, but their ignorance is total and exposes them to the worst blunders.

["No, they are not aviators; scarcely breveted, they no longer fly. 'Goodby crate! Spiders, weave your white webs in my fuselage. For us the Onoto, the Remington, the new Panhard cars, the tactical work.' Scarcely will they make one or two sorties to get a croix or a citation, like a frog who jumps in the air after a red rag. Their plane is the headquarters car, for the ground is an element surer than the wings of the wind. Their work: liaison with supreme headquarters and the biggest brass, paper work, visits to the squadrons where, in carrying out interrogations with a severe air and listening to the good fellows (you remember that grotesque one with a beard who did this to us), they glean the gossip which, spun out, will make circulars and regulations. Their work: be on the lookout for vacancies, to butter-up chiefs, to beg for positions, to gather decorations.

["And aviation has given to the so-called tacticians three inestimable benefits:

["An exceptional advancement.

["The advantage of leaving for a safe job the company or the battery where they might have left their hides.]

"The fine title of aviator which inspires among the naive mass the idea of all courage and all sacrifice."

"Perruche, are you through?"

"No, because I still have to rail against old aviators [who still hang around in some headquarters and whom the old people's home or their branch of origin, artillery or infantry, urgently reclaims, for they cannot or will not fly any longer.]

"When I speak of old aviators, you understand me. I mean those who, having flown but little in peace time, have not done much more in war time; have had their fill of danger September 14 and after that have pontificated in an office. I am not speaking certainly of those swell fellows like Pégoud, Garros, Brindejonc, de Rose, like M. . . . , Pr. . . . , the two M's and P. . . . who have long experience, a resolute courage and still sting the Boche as on the first day. [But for twenty of them we find a hundred others who people the schools and ministries, the supply depots, in short all the safe billets which aviation of the half-front and the rear offers.] Leave aside the technicians; they are necessary; but I know those who are still in the days of the three-cylinder Anzani* and confuse Nieuports with the 28 HP Bleriots of their youth.

"There is a certain justification in saying that they used up their pluck, their nerve, their aggressive qualities before we did; that, captivated by the risk of the sport alone, they have not been able to stand the idea of the added dangers of shells, machine guns, aerial combats. But really the majority have given very little. We could hope that, among the men flying from the very first, we would find an inexhaustible mine of ardent

*A 25 hp engine used to power a Penguin, a training plane with short wings in which French pilots learned to taxi.

chiefs practicing what they preach, ready for all audacities. I have a score of names on the tip of my tongue of those who have greatly disillusioned us. (Alas! These are not the only ones we have admired before the war; but that is another story, and all shirkers find a shelter in war time.)

"I would rather not talk to you (I risk going a bit too far) of those who, having never been much inspired, see the last breath of courage depart:

"Tircis. . . .

"It is time to think of the delights awaiting us in the harbor.*

"They look for a desk job, the sector which in receiving them will allow them to avoid mortar shells, combat, flights over the lines. [When will we see the last of these puppets give way to an elite who will fly on the days of attack, will watch over the range finders, the planes of the command, the pursuit patrols, steel the young with all the authority which experience gives, and sweep out this chair-warming and narrow-minded bureaucracy, capable of preparing, during the hardest hours of the trench war, a great plan for the employment of aviation in the war of movement, as I have seen done during this offensive where our losses were so heavy.]

"To command aviation, we want aviators, nothing but aviators, people who fly less often than the crews, because their work occupies them, but who have flown and know how to fly. We have to know how to get rid of mediocrities. The trouble with us is that we do not know how to give someone

*The lines are from Stanzas to Tircis by Honorat de Recan, lines familiar to all French college students: "Tircis, we must think of drawing back. Our days are more than half spent . . . It is time," etc. J. B. V.

the door. Aviation is not what people think it is, it is infinitely better and infinitely worse; [it is half made up of people who will break their necks and get themselves killed and others who, caring nothing, injure us in profiting by our reputation.] They are foxes disguised in lion's skins, and we are the poor devils of skinned lions.

"When will we have the puppets, the bluffers, the intrigants, the slackers, the blow hards, expelled from among us; those who are ignorant of their profession, live on an usurped reputation, profit from our miseries, make us suffer for their blunders, trample our flowerbeds, monopolize our rewards, dishonor our branch, steal our glory, spoil our finest vines?]

"Drive off, drive off, the little foxes who spoil our vines . . ."

Chatting thus, it took us less than three quarters of an hour to go back to Chalons and to find ourselves comfortably seated and without a care before a cassis and water in the garden of the Hotel d'Angleterre et de Strassbourg. Suddenly the scream of sirens and the noise of 75's made us look up and we could see in the midst of the bursting of shells a squadron of Boche crates which came at three o'clock in the afternoon between 9,000 and 10,000 feet to bomb Chalons.

Aviators victims of aviators, we have seen a lovely raid. The bombs have begun to fall steadily; the streets have emptied themselves as if under a rain storm. As to the hotel cashier, a pretty blonde of Rubens type who an instant before was smiling at us, she has bounded from her counter and run for the cellar clutching the cash box to her bosom and taking time to cry to us in her justified haste:

"It is disgusting to see aviators sitting in a cafe

when the Boches come to murder us. Aren't you ashamed not to be defending us, you wretches!"

The wretches, their pride hurt, could not follow their accuser in her protective cellar, despite their great desire to do so. They thus remained drinking their cassis notwithstanding the shells which fell thick and fast and the pieces of tile which fell even into the garden.

It should be admitted that after a few minutes the pretty blonde, who had some misgivings, had the courage to leave her cellar to beg us to take shelter near the other customers. In face of our dignified refusal she went so far as to make excuses. We were going to follow her, but the raid was already over.

A single seater of the N. . . has shot down one of the bombers, a big L.V.G. two-seater which had launched its six torpedoes and was returning toward its lines as fast as it could. The Nieuport put shots into its wings, but had maneuvered so well that the panic stricken Boche pilot ended by landing behind our lines. The two Germans have been made prisoner with their machine intact.

The L.V.G. has been brought to the airfield before being submitted captive to the curiosity of the Chalonnais; as Peyrussac and I are going to take off in our F.40, finally ready, we see a cortege approach. It is the pilot and the observer who are confronted with their plane.

They arrive stiff and with drawn faces. The observer is a guard officer, the pilot a non-commissioned officer of the Bavarian infantry, who has tears in his eyes.

An army captain dances around them, interrogating them in bad German, asking explanations, demonstrations and clarifications concerning their crate. They refuse to talk; with bad grace they scarcely give a bit of information on the mechanisms which by their simplicity are nothing secret.

One senses the shame, the remorse, the regrets that fill them. They feel that they could have resisted, fought to the end, regained their lines, not have landed foolishly without wounds or damage, avoided being thus submitted to the curiosity of an inglorious crowd of mechanics, motorists, secretaries and commissary men; a humiliation to be followed by so many others which they see before them without end.

Between two reservists they climb back onto a tractor and leave for the town jail.

The slackers sneer, joke, boast. But we cannot help feeling that a similar fate perhaps awaits us, imagining the possible day when, bareheaded, coatless, we might be driven off in the cars of aviators of the other side, be brought, downcast, before our captive plane, now useless, immobile and ridiculous; submitted to the curiosity of a hostile crowd jabbering a strange language, then cut off, abandoned, lost, leave for the prison, like a pauper's grave, toward boredom, cold, hunger, awaited packages, letters which do not arrive . . .

C.R.FROST

A Cassis during Raid

# XI

La Fresnaye* was the oldest pilot of the F.00.
He joined aviation in September, 1914, as a non-commissioned officer observer, became pilot at
the beginning of 1915, and had never left the
squadron, for which he was an example of discipline, courage, and devotion.

He had the finest of service records, among
other things having shot down a Boche over our
lines in a Farman 80 HP.

Adjutant until last September, he contributed to
the maintenance of the best morale among the
non-commissioned officers. Since, he had been
named second lieutenant and we had never had a
finer comrade.

All the F.00 liked and esteemed him. He was the
"veteran."

September 19 the captain sends La Fresnaye to
Bar to get a new plane intended to replace his old
130, celebrated among us for its two red chevrons.

We are sitting in the mess when we see him
return. He does a turn at the end of the field to
make his landing. He has scarcely banked to the
right when his plane unaccountably goes into a
spin and crashes to the ground wing over wing.
We hear the crash of the fall and immediately see
fire and smoke which burst from the debris. It all
happens in the wink of an eye; we do not even
have time to get out of our chairs.

We run, but the accident has taken place at the
other end of the field; when we arrive, the plane
is completely consumed, the passenger, a mechanic, who could not get out, is burned to death. La

*Real name, Duchenois. J. B. V.

Fresnaye, screaming and fighting his uniform covered with flaming gas, is being pulled out of the plane.

We carry him to the hospital at Vadelaincourt which has seen the death of so many aviators. His face, hands, stomach, and legs are terribly burned. Despite the large dose of morphine he is given he suffers horribly. I would never have thought that a man could suffer such martyrdom, and still he speaks, he thanks us, he holds out his hands to us, he speaks the names of his parents, of his brother, a sergeant of Zouaves killed the preceding month.

At eight o'clock in the evening his pain diminishes, the doctor advises us to let him rest. We leave the building and, as we look back a last time at the door the nurse motions for us to return: our comrade is dead . . .

. . . September 21. We have buried Paul-Raymond La Fresnaye and Emile Plateau, his mechanic, killed on the field of Vadelaincourt September 19, 1916, in an accident which we can only blame on their machine.

[La Fresnaye's number two mechanic, who returned from Bar by land, has told us that at the annex they had delivered a new type of plane to our friend. He was a bit anxious to have to pilot a plane of which he did not know the qualities of flight when he left for Vadelaincourt.

[In the week which has followed, the F.00 and the neighboring squadrons have received a certain number of machines of this new type. During this period there have been three fatal accidents and two serious crashes, always with the same planes which inexplicably went into a spin, did not right themselves, and crashed to the ground.

[All of these accidents have terribly shaken the morale of the pilots. We have stopped flying these planes, so bizarre and so dangerous. We have put them under observation, to study their controls and their construction. It is thus that we have been able to spot gross blunders contrary to the most elementary technical rules, and the planes were not even built according to specifications. Moreover, there were differences between planes of the same model.

[We have left the crates in the hangars, made detailed reports supported by figures; we have waited.

[The headquarters of the army, overwhelmed by this series of accidents, backed us up and forwarded our complaints, confirming that the planes of the new type were failures, badly planned, dangerous and unbalanced.

[Here, the story gets lost in mystery and obscurity which the sagacity of a lieutenant pilot of an escadrille cannot pierce. It escapes my competence. By what path have these reports passed? What personages have been called upon to examine them, to decide on the matter, to look for the responsible authorities, to take measures which might avoid repetition of such accidents? To find out it would be necessary to trace back a trail too obscure, give a good shaking to those asleep, expose complaisances, bring to light jobbery and all that for a small, a very small story— the death of a few aviators at the front.

[Two weeks after the departure of the report, two civilians arrived at Vadelaincourt, sent by the firm which had constructed the incriminated planes. Pierre immediately dubbed them "the Jockey" and "the Trainer." Impossible to better describe the infinitely sporting and English manner of the first, his thinness, his shaven face, his half-belted jacket, his bottle-green socks; and the horsy roundness of the second, white cloth cap, store suit, bell-shaped coat, big enough to hide a whole family.

[The role of these two was as follows: the Trainer, an assembly mechanic, would examine the machines and, if need be, have them readjusted, under his eyes, by our personnel; in addition he was full of humbug. The Jockey, a civilian pilot, would receive and check in our presence the crates thus worked on. The two companions affirmed that the defects of these planes were not imputable to the builders; having left the factory in perfect condition, they had been altered and damaged by the military pilots who had had them in their hands before us. May I be permitted not to believe any of this, but in affairs of this kind the main thing is to save face, and the most ridiculous excuse at least has the advantage of assuring a way out.

[The Jockey and the Trainer put themselves to work. Moreover, it was no little thing; we observed the operation. The most bizarre errors were confirmed, the most amazing mistakes of adjustment. If they had been the premeditated act of military pilots, they would have shown deliberate sabotage which would have compounded the crime and the sadism. The planes thus readjusted, the Jockey tested them. He made a level flight around the field and landed, nothing more. Not once did he wish to make a banked turn, no matter how small, a matter of principle, he said, but for us, is it possible to have principles? We must fly our planes in all positions and make vertical turns when shells burst near, or when a Boche presses us too hard.

[Thus the delegate of the builders, the professional, the specialist did not want to put his plane through maneuvers which are daily imposed on us by the necessities of war.

[When the civilians had gone, we had to take our machines and do our work, without joy it is true, in these doubtful planes, for we had no others. The pilot who does not have confidence in his machine, is exactly in the situation of an artilleryman who fears that his cannon will blow up. There is no more demoralizing mental state, and he who would cut a good figure under enemy fire and in the hardest combats, will support with difficulty the fear of seeing himself betrayed by the implement he has in his hands.

[Two weeks later and the story has had its last episode (I do not wish to speak of the death of Captain B. . . who went into a spin and killed himself in one of these very same machines. There you have the logical consequence and not the end of what we relate).

[A young pilot has arrived on the field; we knew of the great reputation for bravery which he has made for himself at the front, first by combat flights, then at the rear in specializing himself in testing new planes. He chose a crate at random and before the assembled camp, in order to give us confidence and drive all fear from our minds, climbed to 4,500 feet and came down in as fancy a spiral as possible.

["You see very well that you can bank these planes," cried the Trainer, returned anew for the occasion.

[I see indeed, I see two things. First of all, the

comrade whose courage and skill I admire will end in a heap. Then, that it was necessary to go get an ace to do acrobatics which the least accomplished pilot can do without danger in a good crate, in a Nieuport for example, but which is exceptionally difficult in a Farman. Now, at present the majority of the Farman pilots we receive at the front are new in the job and of a middling proficiency. They thus have the right to a plane that does not become dangerous as soon as it leaves the hands of stunt fliers and virtuosos.]

We have put La Fresnaye's affairs in order; we have burned his letters, photos, souvenirs, destroyed that which should not go to his family, notified those he had asked to be notified.

At the front, one does not have time to think long about the dead; their memory does not hamper the actions of the living; still, this one, the best, leaves a void, a great void.

I know that as soon as one of us falls, we immediately find a comrade to take his place over the lines and volunteers of all arms to maintain the effectives of the aviation at their fullest; but I think very few will have the head and the heart of Raymond La Fresnaye.

# XII

*Two Days of Victory*

. . . 28 September. The rain falls on the Adrian hut of the F.00. The captain has gathered us around him in his room. Max, sitting sideways on the pine table, leafs through the firing orders, secret notes, detail-maps pencilled in red and blue. Basil and I, leaning against the wall, discuss the attack, smoke, think. Despite this attitude of know-it-alls or of the general staff, First Empire style, we are a small, very small, element in the midst of the offensive which is being prepared.

The army must attack the large German salient which, thrusting as far as Fleury, has menaced Verdun for more than three months. Already along the roads, repaired by a multitude of military work crews, pass materiel, munitions, artillery and troops, all the elements of the enormous push which should free Verdun and perhaps recapture the forts whose loss has been so bitter for us—the forts of Vaux and Douaumont.

Ever since the offensive of the Somme has reduced Verdun to the role of a secondary theater, our planes have resisted the German planes as well as they could; each has about balanced out the other, but now we see air forces flowing to our army which will give us a crushing superiority over the Boches.

The attack is expected to occur in the middle of October. While the infantry prepares the jump-off trenches, batteries and more batteries are being set up on the banks of the Meuse and of the canal, behind the fort of Vacherauville, on the hillside of Belleville and even in the suburbs of

Verdun. As for us, we increase our artillery spotting, photo taking, destruction of batteries, visual reconnaissance; we devote ourselves to the minute study of the terrain where we must work.

. . . 10 October. On ten kilometers of the front shells of all calibers pound the trenches, the shelters, the communication trenches, the ammunition dumps, the tracks and especially the batteries. These latter, assailed by an artillery infinitely superior, are silenced and submit to shelling under which cannon and personnel must dissolve and the casemates and entrenchments be crushed.

A multitude of planes is constantly artillery spotting over the lines; the enemy aviation does not dare respond. Our pursuit squadrons, disciplined, organized, energetically commanded, assure us complete security and their mastery over the Boche is now absolute. The planes of the Army Corps which fly at all altitudes and often quite far into enemy territory do not have to face a combat; on the other hand the guns of the armored cars submit them to serious fire and we fly through numerous explosions of 77's and 105's.

Yesterday, as I piloted Max for artillery spotting in the region of Thiaumont, a 105 shell exploded near us in a large greenish puff. Max leaning over his transmitter, suddenly fell head first to the bottom of the cockpit. Riveted to my seat by my belt, I thought for an instant that my friend was killed before my eyes.

He remained several seconds without moving, then he stirred, shook himself, straightened up, lifted his hand to the nape of his neck and showed me a large shell splinter, which, its force spent, had come to rest in the cork lining of his helmet. He got off with a shock and a bruise, but immediately returned to his spotting saying: "I thought you'd given me a heavy blow with your fist." Then we returned to circling among the trench mortars.

. . . 21 October. We have strenuous work which the very rainy bad weather of this month of October constantly hinders. We are obliged to fly under the lowest ceilings, take advantage of the slightest openings, return only when the rain has really started to fall. We see pilots land under the rain who have had to take off their befogged goggles and whose flying togs are shining like a sou 'wester.

The attack anticipated for tomorrow is put off because the weather has delayed artillery spotting; nevertheless tons of shells fall on the enemy. Twilight has brought a break in the weather which has allowed the planes to take off in numbers. Some only returned at nightfall to the field lit by large gasoline fires. We were among the last to arrive. In the obscurity we could see the lines crackling with explosions and numberless bursts; the burning ammunition dumps light up the darkness of the ravines. It was the fantastic vision of the immense forge of Verdun.

A cannon of 400 fires on the forts. We envy the comrades to whose lot has fallen the direction of the fire of this monster. To deliver such projectiles on the Boche! We see enormous shells fall on Douaumont; the shell hole is dug, the spray of debris, dirt, rocks spatters all of the fort, then the noise of the powerful explosion reaches us.

Suddenly Max sticks out his arm. A stronger detonation shakes Douaumont, rolls and amplifies itself. Heavy black smoke boils up in the center of the fort, slowly curls up, and spreads out in a mushroom, 3000 feet high, the color of soot, which the wind slowly carries toward the west. The fort has blown up. A shell of the 400 searching to the bottom of a casemate stuffed with projectiles and explosives must have set off in the underground passages an indescribably horrible scene of destruction, asphyxiation and death.

An hour later the wind from the Meuse has borne away the immense cloud, draws it out, lengthens it in the form of an interminable S for more than fifteen kilometers and carries it to spread the news of the disaster among the enemy.

We have likewise seen the fort of Vaux blown up, but we were farther away and could not see the work of our big guns as distinctly; nevertheless we did see the same plume of black smoke, heavy and thick, covering the fort with a funereal pall.

. . . 23 October. The attack is set for tomorrow morning, but we do not know, so thick is the fog, so menacing is the weather, if we can take part. Basil, with Gilbert, is designated to follow the progress of the infantry; before the attack others will direct rapid fire of gas shells on the artillery and the reserves; still others (including Max and me) will follow each other over the lines to locate the enemy batteries in action and to direct counter fire against them.

. . . 24 October. The wind has turned to the west and spread a cottonlike fog a hundred feet or so above the ground. We are up very early in the morning, and the breath of cold and humid air which greets us at the window lets us know at once that the weather has turned bad. We wait on pins and needles the hour of the attack without the sky clearing. The fog continues to envelop us and cuts off visibility at a few yards. The artillery spotting planes do not take off, but those for infantry liaison, without worrying about the clouds and the deplorable visibility, take off in the fog at the fixed hour.

A few moments later, lured by a vague break, we also take off, hoping to find a hole over the lines which will permit us to work.

Air borne, we maneuver between patches of fog which at times go down to the level of the trees and twine among their tops, sometimes rise to 300 feet and cease to bother us. Suddenly the hill of Froideterre looms up in front of us. Its summit is in the cloud, its foot in the mist coming up from the Meuse. The big hill is surrounded by a belt of fire and of noise caused by countless flashes, by strident crashes, by the mad miauling of hundreds of guns which scream and spit in the paroxysm of the attack which is let loose. The sharp rapid flashes make holes in the fog and the fury of the detonations seems to hurl itself in vain at the white wall which rises in front of the guns. We had to get past these batteries, fly among the projectiles which tore the air around us, and in the mist which covers us with a veil, vague, shifting, impenetrable.

A breach opens to us, we try to pass through, but immediately the hole closes and we circle, lost for an instant, shaken, surrounded by shell fire, brushing a hill crest, exposing our backs to

[121]

the next shell which will hit us in the middle and end our futile flight.

A Nieuport passes very near, a large fly gone astray like us, which misses hitting us, already fading into the gray while we are still frightened at seeing it so close.

Very low we fly over the deadly circle of the batteries to return to the field. The infantry planes have remained. What could Basil have done? Why has he not yet returned? At noon we are without news from him; at 12:30 still nothing and our concern mounts. At 12:45 the telephone rings for the thousandth time, Max runs to answer and the following dialog takes place:

"This is Castillon."*

"This is Basil."

"Ah! old man, are you hurt?"

"No."

"Where are you?"

"At the Fort de Mare."

"What happened to you?"

And here is his account:

"We were shot down. We left close to ground level with the infantry. The riflemen were so happy to see us fifty feet over head that they waved their helmets in leaving for the assault and shouted bravo, clapping their hands; but obviously, because of our speed, we went past them. The fog thickened again and the crate almost crashed into the hillside of Froideterre; then we got lost. We flew without direction; the big shells exploding below riddled us with shell splinters; a fort, probably Haudromont, machine-

*True name, Sourdillon. See note, p. 24.

gunned us; we made a half turn toward the south. The riflemen advanced in groups and the Germans in front of them retreated from shell hole to shell hole; some however stopped in clusters, islets of resistance. In a crater a dozen Boches crouched. I circled around them and fired with my Colt machine gun and they answered with rifle shots. There was a loud noise in my motor; a bullet had hit a piston rod. Still the motor turned over at 800 or 900 r.p.m. and Gilbert was able to get us here. The crate is in shreds; we are unhurt. We will be back tonight."

At four o'clock the ceiling lifts, we see large blue holes while scarfs of fog still trail to the ground and from time to time turn into rain or sleet. All of the planes of Vadelaincourt take off one after the other. We leave also. The guns are still firing heavy bursts but already the batteries of 75's are leaving their positions and advancing toward the north. We are again in the path of the shells, but it makes no difference now that we can fly high, whereas this morning we were flying right in front of the muzzles of the guns. The lines are very far away, seven or eight kilometers beyond the jump-off trenches; the fire from the German barrage extends its bursts and its smoke over more than a kilometer to the north of Douaumont and above Vaux.

The deep zone of our advance is upheaved, turned up as if by a ploughshare. I never imagined such devastation, complete, profound, thorough, nothing has escaped; the shell holes do not touch each other, they overlap. Neither trench nor woods, nor house nor road can be distinguished; Fleury is so completely pounded that not a trace of it can be found.

It is the turn of German guns to fire on Douaumont. The Boches have evacuated the fort and already a path marks the entrance of our troops. Shells of very large caliber fall on the half destroyed fort, completing the disaster of the ravaged superstructure and the filled moats.

Max, leaning over his transmitter, exerts himself to the utmost. He is the artilleryman possessed. Everywhere enemy gun flashes light up. On those which he locates, he calls down a rain of projectiles. He is completely wrapped up in his work, which excites and transports him. He thinks neither of the shells whose passing shakes us up, nor of the hail which at times whips our faces.

Above us the rays of the sun glide between the clouds, irridescent in the rain, and an immense rainbow is thrown against the vertical storm clouds which trail toward the earth in white scarfs.

I seem to see the circles of Dante, limbo crowned with the glory of the sky, while below the explosions, the flames, the upheaval appear the smoking horror of hell. The plane, the only human thing, sharply defined, solid and real, supports us, carries us half way between this radiance and this desolation.

. . . 25 October. Verdun is freed. We have retaken the principal circle of its defenses; Fort Thiaumont and Fort Douaumont have been carried in the attack of yesterday. Today, Fort de Vaux has fallen. The capture of 7000 prisoners and about a hundred pieces of artillery is announced.

. . . December. All night on the road which borders our field we have heard uninterrupted rumbling of the trucks, going up to the lines with the troops who will attack.

The army of Verdun wants to expand its success of October, to mount an offensive which for good and for all will push the Germans out of range of the town. The attack is being prepared. Why shouldn't it have the same success as the first? But this time it is necessary to bring up troops and artillery, transport munitions and supplies over a zone of eight kilometers, chewed up by shells, where roads, beaten paths, and even communication trenches are lacking.

Still everything is getting organized: paths multiply; troops work; guns small and large move up, Lord knows how, over chaotic ground and place themselves in unsheltered positions. Roads are retraced in this desert and the Decauville railroad brings materiel almost to the first line.

And the troops continue to come up; the road is encumbered by a flood of blue or khaki uniforms. When we are not flying, we look, with emotion, at this tragic defile; sections pass, mingling faces too young with those bearded and already mature. The officers are in front, canes under their arms, helmets on their heads, dressed in the same faded blue as their men. The thin and grave faces of some reflect a sort of haughty and fierce pride and seem to say: ["While we go toward the attack, bowed under a discipline anonymous and inflexible as destiny, half of France laughs, amuses itself, gets rich, threatens demoralization for lack of a scrap of white bread or a lump of sugar; half the army shirks, intrigues, wins crosses and honors, and the carelessness of some, the ambition of others rests on our obscure, relentless and superhuman effort . . ."]

What to answer? We are ashamed of our clean uniforms and our dry huts, of our nights of rest. And we almost want to abandon the profession which we love, follow them, join the ill-humored crowd, pitiful and magnificant who are going to fight the hardest and most glorious of combats.

The sky is a fine dappled gray. From the ground the clouds seem to be at a thousand feet, but one can climb up to ten or twelve thousand toward the veil which hides the sun and the visibility is as good as over the mountains the day before rain.

Artillery preparation continues. Cannon is king here. There is not a square yard of enemy lines which has not been hit by a shell, not a battery which has not been crushed, not a trench which has not been wiped out, not a shelter whose entrance is not caved in or which has not been invaded by gas. And on this terrain, men, Boches, live. They try to eat, to sleep, to drink from streams or from ruined springs whose water seeps in yellowish puddles into the mud of shell craters. They service their guns, bring up supplies, munitions, orders. Confident until now in their own strength, they must be frightened before the irresistible manifestation of ours.

. . . 15 December. The weather is good, without rain or frost. The clouds are at about 4500 feet; at eight o'clock we know that planes can cooperate in the attack.

With Max we must carry out a counter battery at the hour of the assault. We take off and an instant later we are in the fight. The artillery is as powerful, perhaps more so, than at the last attack; its fire is uninterrupted and the planes which fly over the battle field are in the midst of innumerable passing shells. Each firing shatters our hearing and seems about to send the shell which, making a direct hit, will blow our Farman to bits. Several times we see the shining metal of a projectile which is hastening towards its distant target. We imagine its course, its rapid climb, then at the top of its trajectory, the pause while it dominates the immense landscape, and finally the swish when it plunges into the emptiness where its fall accelerates; each detonation shakes us in our seats and, with bent backs, contorted faces, nerves taut, we await the fatal issue of the last shell.

We ask ourselves if we can stay five minutes in this furrowed air; yet like fifty others we have remained three hours, and the danger was doubtless not so great, for few were lost, at least in this manner.

Lurking everywhere, in the ravines, in the orchards, in the stripped woods, even in the shell holes of the jump-off trenches, without the shelter of a sap or of a simple trench, the 75's grow hoarse and impatient and fire continuously. There is a whole pack of them which, grouped behind the fort of Vacherauville, howls with an access of fury when an objective is suddenly revealed. Single or coupled mastiffs, the heavy guns, numerous, powerful, irresistible, bay out with a duller and deeper voice. Everywhere tongues of fire dart out, and even Douaumont, ravaged, lost and retaken, still fires with its turrets which ten months of combat have not destroyed.

The German artillery reacts, but wearily and sporadically. It does not know where its infantry is, it is blind, for its planes, pursued by our pilots, prowl around the battle field without being able to reach it. On the other hand, the anti-aircraft guns pursue us relentlessly and no one will land without shell-splinters in his wings. Don't think of those who will be shot down. The machine guns from the ground fire on us energetically; the low flying infantry planes of which very few are armored, are really catching it. Some have their motor hit but, still turning over a bit, are able to reach the flat land of the Meuse or the field at Verdun. The sudden stopping of their motor forces others to hit the ground where they are and to flip over in the shell holes, to the greater or less injury of the passengers. And finally the pilot and observer are sometimes killed in the air and it is a pure and simple crash. More than thirty planes are out of action on the battle field, some with almost no damage and others completely wrecked. Spads, Nieuports, G.4's and Farmans are friendly neighbors with a broken wing, wheels in the air, or nosed over.

Our work is finished. For three hours flying in the midst of this inferno, above the battle,* but playing our role in it and exposed to all the repercussions of exploding shells, we used our radio, helped the artillerymen, called down on the Boches a storm of projectiles. Max gives me the sign that we can land; I shout to him, "Shall we go down and

*An allusion to Romain Rolland's *Above the Battle (Au dessus de la mêlée)*, published in Switzerland. The book scandalized the troops at the front. J. B. V.

take a look?" "Down we go," he answers. I cut my throttle and spiral to within 150 feet of the ground.

Far to the north of our lines of this morning, our troops march slowly on broken ground. At times a shrapnel or a percussion shell explodes in their midst, but the enemy fire is neither intense nor exact. Planes follow them. From time to time, when the progress stops, the signal flares mark out the new front. Behind this first wave the support troops also advance—these are Zouaves. They come to a halt behind a crest, hear the noise of our motor, lift their heads and wave. The colonial troops in their mustard-colored uniforms line themselves up as if at maneuvers. In a shell hole five or six poilus wave us a hello. A 150 explodes in the middle of them, surrounds them with smoke and dust, and when the cloud is lifted, limp forms are spread out in the shell hole. But already the khaki line gets up and moves toward the north.

We leave the Zouaves, we leave the ravines with bizarre names—ravine de la Dame, ravine de la Couleuvre, ravine du Helly—which the artillery has devastated, which, overrun by the assault waves, are still more desolated in their solitude. Now the terrain is populated. Artillery reinforcements advance, lines of reservists bring up munitions; wounded are returning, held up by their comrades; the stretchers pass.

In the hollow where Fleury used to be, something is crawling—a long greenish line winds; other similar lines come down from Douaumont. These are, eight abreast, unarmed men, prisoners, prisoners, hundreds of prisoners. The wounded conduct them: Zouaves, black riflemen, infantrymen, whose bandages we can see. They push this docile and resigned herd in front of them. In a little while these Boches will realize their dream; they will enter Verdun, but as captives and with lowered heads.

Max turns toward me. I think he is crying. Is it the fatigue, the jangled nerves, the physical let down after the danger and the noise? One thing for sure, it is not sentimentalism, for fliers cannot cry, as tears fog up goggles and aviators have to keep sharp vision.

Still, we have made our effort, we have played our part, small it is true, but our part, and here before our eyes is our recompense.

We can well feel some emotion, because to-night, our obscure and modest task accomplished, it is given us to fly in a victorious sky.

# XIII

"Verdun, Verdun!" sings the car which carries me toward Bar. Sitting between Max and Peyrussac I am leaving Verdun, Verdun, my whole life as a pilot, the soldier aviator, all of my battle.

Verdun, Verdun. The noise of the car makes this tragic name echo in my head. Who will know what these two syllables will represent for those who have fought here? Verdun—the fallen comrades; Verdun—the multitude of fantastic visions, of emotions, of enthusiasms, of dangers, of fatigue, of agony; Verdun—retreat, resistance, victories.

Verdun, Verdun. You others who have not defended it, you will never know what the name Verdun is for us.

"Old man, you are leaving, you are going to pilot a pursuit plane; you are deserting us," says Max.

"For you the single-seater, a Nieuport or a Spad; for you to bring down the Boches instead of being shot down," says Peyrussac.

Bar. They shake hands and give me a fraternal embrace.

"Well, old man, you are leaving us at the front, you are going to the rear?"

"Not for long, I hope."

"You will tell them a bit of what you have seen, those behind the lines. They don't know what our war is . . . the civilians and the shirkers!"

Tell them, tell them what? Tell them what we have seen, what we have done? That's too easy, not fantastic or romantic enough; that will not divert anyone. The pilots of the rear have accustomed their listeners to much finer stories, spiced with a slang which I don't know. They know how to talk of fierce combats, slipstreams and storms, loops, banks and slides. What would I have of this kind to tell?

And then there is a firm belief which will never leave the civilians and a good number of military that their aviators are a kind of tight rope walkers, harum scarum fellows, mechanics; and who will believe me when I say that, among all my friends and comrades of front line aviation, I never met any but soldiers.

# Part Two

*N. 705 The Fighter Escadrille**

*The Story of 12 Single-Seaters.*

*Actually N. (Nieuport) 102, later SPA (Spad) 102. J. B. V.

Fighter pilot.

Here end reports, long-winded lectures, oral or written embellishments of the truth. Our losses and our victories speak for themselves.

Only one thing is important—knock down the Boche.

Is there a combatant as solitary as we?

Twelve or fourteen thousand feet; a pilot who rocks his single-seater; a machine gun; two hundred rounds; all the space in the world to fly in, all the Boches to attack if we feel belligerent and to knock down if we can . . .

# I

*The airfield at Lépinois.*

. . . 22 February. The chance to which I trusted myself at Plessis-Belleville has served me well. It sent me to the air field at Lépinois, to N. 705 under the orders of Bertrand,* cavalry lieutenant, who was my comrade and neighbor during our time at Vadelaincourt.

N. 705 is a squadron of single-seaters; twelve pilots (three officers, nine non-commissioned officers), twelve planes (six Spads and six Nieuports). Our mission is pursuit in the sector and from time to time protection of photo reconnaissance, at long range towards Laon, La Fère, Chauny or Saint-Quentin.

"For the time being, you will take a Nieuport, 1723, which has just been overhauled. The first Spad to arrive is for Loris, the next will be for you. As for flying . . ."

Bertrand indicates the foul weather.

Lépinois is 22 kilometers southwest of Soissons. A large plateau where the beet fields, fallow since the war, serve us as a landing field. It is terrain open to the four winds but still not so bad, for there is room to land and take off. At present

---

*Lt. Derode, a remarkable officer who, after seven or eight aerial victories, was killed at the end of 1917. He was my friend and commander of the escadrille. J. B. V.

the thaw makes it soft, slippery and dangerous for propellors. My new boss takes me around the cantonment of the squadron. The three Bessonneaus full of planes are closed and dark. In an Adrian hut are the mechanics, and the office. In another are the pilots, in small rooms. I shake hands with my future companions. Three of them are presented to me who are the best of the squadron: Chelcher* plays piquet with Piston, while de Loris carves a potato masher from a joy stick,** for he is mess officer.

The officers, Bertrand, Lamajou and I, are lodged in an abandoned sugar beet factory which borders the road. Our rooms under the roof and over the work floor are glacial, but the oil stoves make them almost habitable. It rains in from time to time; the furniture is of unpainted wood, made by the mechanics.

The officers mess in the kitchen of the former caretaker of the farm is a bit isolated but friendly; the evening invariably brings bridge filled out sometimes by one of our non-commissioned officers or by an officer from the neighboring R.4.


. . . February. I am strapped tightly into a 15 meter,*** 110 hp. Octave, promoted to the rank of rotary mechanic, cries: "Cut?" Cut! "Contact?" Contact! The Le Rhone engine turns over and whines with the sound of crumpled steel leaves, as one might say.

---

*Cadet Bamberger, a good and brave pilot. Invalided out of service, he volunteered for aviation. He survived the war and died of illness after. J. B. V.

**Slang for the control stick of a plane; literally "broom stick"(manche à balai).

***Fifteen square meters of wing surface.

Control stick forward, the tail lifts, a few bounces on the bumps of the field and the ground sinks away.

Piston has given me rendezvous at 3000 feet over the hangars. From there we streak off over the lines while continuing to climb.

There the Aisne flowing east-west will serve us as a major point of reference. Here is Soissons which the Boches and the French dispute; the Cliffs of the Aisne; the deep ravines stretching toward the north and where so many battles have occurred; the forest of Compiègne where I was a recruit in peace time;* the forest of Laigle, and the Oise which winds toward Noyon.

We continue to climb. At nine thousand we dive on Crapeaumesnil where we draw a few shells, then we return toward the east, rocking our planes in the cold air.

I dip my left wing in order to see below me if a Boche is not coming up, hidden by my wing, then my right to take another look. A sharp turn and climb to the left, twisting my neck to see behind and above me always to prevent surprise. And during this time, to regulate the carburetion, I am fiddling with the red handled throttle and the bright colored mix lever.

Twelve thousand feet. Piston turns in every direction above a countryside which I do not recognize. I follow him and become completely disoriented, as much because the earth is covered with a light haze, as that the ceiling three thousand feet above us hides the sun, and night is about to fall.

We have been flying for an hour and a quarter.

*I began my military career as a dragoon at Compiègne in 1911. J. B. V.

Not a sign of a Boche. We must be near the extremity of the forest of Compiègne, but all these woods confuse me.

My motor starts to sputter; I handle the Le Rhone badly for it is still new to me. It would be better to return. I dive toward what I think is our lines.

Five minutes; a large town over there, it must be Compiègne; from there I will fly up the river toward Soissons. Ten minutes; a town. It is not the Compiègne I am familiar with and that I saw a while ago. There is a river with its banks largely overflowing, a bizarre garden, no junction of streams. My motor is still missing. Where can I be?

Circling over the city which I do not want to lose sight of, I try to orient myself on my map; the sun is hidden, and I do not dare rely on my compass; I am ill at ease; squeezed in a single-seater I am not used to, I do not see clearly. I am a little anxious.

At my altitude, a crate appears and approaches. A Boche? I arm my machine gun. Another instrument I am not familiar with. I also do not know how to use it very well, because the Lewis is fixed in the axis of the plane and it is necessary to aim with the whole machine, a bit of acrobatics for which I feel myself still quite inexperienced.

But seeing a red gleam on the wings, I recognize the cockades of a Frenchman; it is Piston himself, who is doubtless hunting for me.

With relief I glue myself to him and we retrace the route taken earlier.

This time there is really the Aisne, Soissons, our Bessonneaus. We lose altitude, we land.

Piston gets out of his crate, comes towards me, his flying togs stiff with frost.

"Excuse me for having lost you, Lieutenant, but you were a long way off course."

"It's my fault, Piston. But what is that place where you came to bail me out?"

"Saint-Quentin . . ."

My first patrol.

. . . February. "There are no Boches in the region," Bertrand tells me, "or rather there are very few, or else you would not have made your promenade with impunity, day before yesterday, 45 or 50 kilometers into their territory. To find any here, one must hunt them to hell and gone or fall on one at the right moment who is making a tour of the sector, takes his photo rapidly and leaves. Usually they are not very aggressive.

"If the sector livens up, that will not last. The squadrons in front of us will come up and we will have to fight every day. For the time being, it is to your advantage to get used to the single-seater before having to do hard work in an area full of Fritz.

"I am getting a Spad from Bourget, do you want it?"

"Certainly."

"Agreed then; you will have a Spad."

. . . February. The weather has been bad all day. Evening reveals the horizon for an instant. The ceiling is still at 3000 feet in places, while in others plenty of sky can be seen. The sun will set in a quarter of an hour. Is it worthwhile to take off?

Standing around the field, we discuss it, officers and non-commissioned officers together. The chief declares that there are not any Boches flying at these hours and he does not want his crates landing at night in this mess.

Immediately in answer to this we hear distant explosions and see white flakes over Soissons. With binoculars we see a plane quietly doing its reconnaissance in the twilight.

Cries of rage from the squadron.

"Chelcher, if you want to team up with me tomorrow we will ambush the Fritz from the corner of a cloud . . ."


. . . February. Bertrand says to me:

"Come make a flight with me. We will try to get a Boche and at the same time we will see the patrols of the squadron at work."

At nine thousand feet over the lines our two Spads make several Mefeus uneasy. We fly along the trenches to the Oise. A swing around Noyon and we fly to the east. At the forest of Saint-Gobain, a turn toward the north as far as the flooded Oise. Twelve thousand feet below us, Chauny and its factories.

Something over there . . . its a Fritz; he sees us coming and says to himself: "I am 30 kilometers behind my lines, these people certainly are not going to attack me here."

But Bertrand does not hesitate; he dashes in his direction.

Hey! boss, you are going a bit far, we can no longer see our trenches. We are completely up against it. Even with two against one, it will be an uneven fight. The Boche holds all the cards; he is in his own territory, while for us . . . a bullet in the tank, in the radiator, in a tail pipe, and we will have had it, and we would have to land here. And then, there are also the other German fliers who can pop up suddenly, while we are busy with this one.

But, Bertrand doesn't think so. Have at the Boche, and full speed ahead!

The plane is very close; it is a two-seater with an in-line engine, small, fast, with green and brown camouflage; two machine guns, one firing through the propellor, the other in the turret.

Bertrand takes an aim on him, his Vickers clatters, then suddenly complete silence . . . , the boss has jammed.

He makes a steep bank and breaks off combat.

It is my turn. I get the Boche in my sight, and diving on him full speed, I let loose a burst. "Tac, tac". The lever of the breech jumps in front of me, and suddenly stops. Jammed!

The Boche does not take long to profit from his advantage. He gains a bit of altitude and dives on me. His Maxim spits, incendiary shells whine around my ears leaving long white trails in the sky. Decidedly, I am in a bad spot; a zoom, a kick of my foot, my Spad is in a spin; six hundred feet lower, having shaken off the Boche, I unjam my machine gun and catch my breath.

During this time Bertrand has returned to the combat. The two crates speed towards one another and fire face to face . . . Good Lord! they are going to crash into each other! No! only a few yards apart, both of them spin dive to miss each other; the camouflaged plane with black crosses and the cream colored Spad with cockades turn parallel to each other; before the Fritz has time to get his balance, I try to get in a burst and Bertrand joins me; the Boche dives, and breaks off the contact. In fleeing, his gunner fires his last shots at us. He disappears and we remain masters of the field. We bank around a couple of times to mark our triumph, then we speed off toward Soissons.

Bertrand has seven or eight balls in his fuselage and his wheels. I have one in my aileron.

My first combat in a single-seater.

. . . February. "The Sopwith will be waiting at 13 hours 9000 feet over Soissons.

"Itinerary of the photo reconnaissance: Laon, La Fère, Saint-Quentin, Tergnier, Chauny and return."

Four Spads are to accompany the flight, but at take off Sagny has trouble with his temperature and we are only three—Chelcher, Piston and I, to escort the two-seater.

The Sop, 9000 feet over Soissons, circles quietly, exactly on rendezvous. We surround him. Piston 600 feet above him, Chelcher and I at his sides. He heads toward the north and we fly over the lines.

Some cannon shots 3000 feet too low (the Sop is taken for a single-seater and the Boche artillerymen make an error in their range). Faster than the Sop, we amuse ourselves, circling, passing him up, grazing close enough to see the passenger in yellow helmet leaning in his cockpit, photographing through a hole in the fuselage between his feet.

Laon, La Fère. Beneath us is a wide expanse of fields, forests, valleys, plateaus. We are very far from our lines; we have already been away twenty-five minutes and there is still half an hour to fly over the enemy.

If my motor cuts out . . .

The 140 Hispano* turns over regularly. The temperature and pressure are steady—950 rpm.

A drop of water in the gasoline. One, two seconds, the motor coughs; some sputtering . . . am I stuck, good Lord? No, it catches.

Is my motor making a funny sound? Something grinding? Nothing but imagination. I have to brace myself not to magnify a merely speculative damage. But still, what anxiety if my motor stopped! At thirty kilometers within enemy territory, with our lines still visible where there is freedom and safety, if I came down with a dead propellor, my motor suddenly silent, on this seemingly calm and familiar land, and where I do not have the right to set down . . .

Saint-Quentin cut by a canal. The twin-seater turns and finally goes back toward the south. We are at 12,500; an east southeast wind makes us deviate a bit and delays our return.

On our left, three dots, three Boches? We approach and they await us. Do they want to bar our passage? The silhouettes become defined. They are clearly Fritz. Ailerons projecting, thick cigar-shaped fuselage, a stocky aspect, somber camouflage, and I don't know what else which leaves no room for doubt.

We close in around the two-seater. We must not let our charge be roughed up.

Fortunately, the Boches do not attack; despite the insult of our presence so far within their lines, they circle around us without approaching,

*Hispano-Suiza

[145]

with the air of peevish fish, disturbed and circumspect.

The Sop starts to descend and rapidly picks up speed. Over the lines, we leave him with a wave of the hand to return to our Bessonneaus.

We land and Piston, standing up in his fuselage, shouts:

"I was jammed from the start. You can imagine the long face I pulled when I saw the Fritz and thought we would have to tangle with them!"

# II

. . . March. The sun still sets very early, the weather is bad every other day, we have very long hours of boredom to pass tied down on our plateau. No village of any kind nearby where we can go relax and traditionally "pay court to the proprietress of the pastry shop."

Our only resources are within ourselves, officers of all ranks are elbow to elbow. Discipline does not suffer but on the contrary there is born a mutual confidence, indispensable for those called to fight side by side, for among us the chiefs are also participants in action; not always the most skilled and successful of pilots, they must be the most conscientious and the bravest; they must assert themselves by their character and their spirit of devotion.

Our officers must be born leaders of men. If they do not have a superior morale, if they are not ready to set the example in all circumstances, they have nothing to do among us. Show them the door, send them to the thousand shelters in the rear or to their original branch, but do not leave them in a front-line escadrille.

For too long certain squadron chiefs have maintained that their functions prevented them from flying. While their pilots were tangling with the Boche, they stayed on the ground to see that motors were repaired or to count their Bessonneaus. The chiefs of the young aviation know their role better.

Thank the Lord! Bertrand knows how to take it out of himself. He has done a lot and knows his job better than any among us; thus he has great authority; demanding and at times peppery, he is loved and admired by all. He is the boss, the chief of the band.

I have always thought that to the extent that the officer is worthy, so are the troops. In pursuit flying, this rule does not absolutely apply, for the squadron once airborne, is no longer under direct command. The pilot, left to himself, has to depend on his individual resources. Nevertheless under a poor chief a good squadron will fall apart rapidly; under a high-level man a normal squadron becomes a first rank unit which knocks down the Boche and loses few people, which is the ideal result.


. . . March. Chelcher lands beautifully and rolls up to the hangars.

"What happened to you?"

His right wing is torn in four places and a broken rib pushes out of the canvas; a strut is severed; the fuselage looks as if it had been sliced with a knife.

"Bullets? What a battering you must have taken!"

"My gas tank also got it. I got back on my auxilliary tank."

"Where did that happen?"

"Ten kilometers north of Soissons. I took off alone to tease the Fritz. At 9000 I saw an old wagon coming quietly toward our lines. I dived on him, but even before I could fire, I heard two machine guns behind me; there were two single-seaters who had hidden in a cloud and who jumped me from above. I saw my canvas tearing. Zing, zing in my ears. A grinding in the motor and my pressure has fallen.

"While doing clever things to get myself out of this, I pumped by hand, and as I got no results, I turned on the emergency tank and came back with the three gallons of emergency fuel."

"You've really done something there. Your crate is completely shot and you'll have to go to Bourget to get another. The supply depot there ought to be good for something."

. . . March. Following the usual custom, we join the Sop over Soissons and, grouped around him, we fly over the lines between nine and ten thousand feet.

Our reconnaissance assignment is to look in the forest of Saint-Gobain for the famous fall-back line which has been so much talked about for several days.

To fall back! If the Boches are doing this, it is that they really cannot do otherwise, for it will make a devil of a stir when a line that has been stable for two and a half years moves for the first time.

In any event, we are looking for the line.

Above the trenches we see a heavy fog over the country extending before us. No, it's not fog, it's smoke. A large low cloud covers an enormous reach of territory. The centers of the fire are especially numerous on the vast plain to the east of the Saint-Quentin-Soissons line. It seems as if all the countryside is on fire. Is it because the Boche wants to evacuate and burn everything behind him?

The observer in the twin seater must note the towns and villages in flames and I don't bother with this work. Meanwhile I see the big fires at Tergnier, Chauny, Saint-Simon, Guiscard, not to mention innumerable small hamlets.

The twin-seater rapidly gains its objectives and hastens to return to the field. It is in a hurry to tell what it has seen and to announce this important news.

Just when it is making a half turn toward Chauny, three planes coming from the west fly in our direction, dancing in the sun like mosquitoes in a ray of light. Chelcher wiggles his taxi to warn me but I have already seen the newcomers. They approach. We distinguish the characteristic silhouette of the Nieuports. Unequal wings, arched fuselage, little rudders in shape of a comma, without tail fins. We relax. The comrades pass us, a bit higher than we. On the fuselage of the closest, whose pilot waves me hello, I distinguish the red plumed hat which is the insigne of the N. . . .

The lines. We cast a last glance on the landscape fifty kilometers wide by eighty long, the four corners of which the Boches have set on fire.

We land and we explain at length to our comrades what we have seen.

. . . March. Very early this morning the sky was superb, now it is closing in; ceiling at 1200 feet. Nothing for us to do. We leave the single-seaters in their stalls.

The phone rings: "Get two pilots of the 705 to fly over the lines at low altitude, from Soissons to Fontenoy. They will push some distance into enemy territory to see if the trenches are occupied."

When we receive this order we are huddled up in the Adrian mess hut, so cold that we are reduced to using heat from a noisy soldering lamp.

"As an ex-pilot of a two-seater, you are certainly it."

I leave to look for a volunteer who wants to go with me. Piston volunteers.

"As for low altitude, we'll have it; the ceiling is less than 1200 feet."

The leaden clouds, with soft contours, drag along the ground. We take off.

We fly along the front. Not a movement. Not a cannon shot. In the trenches nothing is visible, which does not surprise us. The first lines always have a desert aspect for us. Actually, except during infantry liaison, aviators never see anyone in the trenches.

Once or twice, Piston, then I, make a circuit of a few kilometers into the territory of the Boche, who does not favor us with so much as shrapnel or a gun shot.

Is it because they have left, all of those people?

We dive to use our machine guns, still without seeing anyone. It is not sporting to fire on rocks. We turn around toward the base. But, busy with our anti-infantry exercises, we have not noticed a heavy black cloud which rolls a somber scroll clear to the ground and bars our route. It starts to snow.

A Spad flies rapidly. I scarcely have time to

C.R FROST

Lost in a Snow Storm

think. I have often flown in the rain, I can certainly try to fly though snow. Away we go! Already the flakes sting my face, and all at once I enter into obscurity.

A white obscurity. I no longer see the earth; scarcely the tips of my wings. I no longer know if I am listing or flying straight. I don't know where I am going and I am at 500 feet!

My windshield is clouding over, my goggles are crusted with ice, and I rip them off; my burning eyes cry and I hide my dripping face in the cockpit.

I am very frightened. Piston has disappeared on my right, I no longer see my compass, for it is dark in my cockpit. All of this is going to end, at 170 kilometers an hour, with a pretty crack up.

I must have pushed the stick without knowing it; suddenly something vague looms up in front of me; without having time to think I pull back the stick with a big jerk and find that I have jumped over the poplars of the Aisne into which I was going to fly.

Full throttle, I climb to escape the dangerous ground. I make a half turn just on a chance; but does one know where he is going in this white whirlwind? From time to time I distinguish the ground which flits beneath me. Two or three minutes more and I fly out of the clouds as rapidly as I entered. Day returns as if I had raised a curtain. I am at three hundred feet. The line of trees of the Aisne is on my right, I am thus within our lines, out of the mess. I had been in the snow cloud for about five minutes.

The sudden snow flurry continues to advance northeast-southwest. There is no reason for me to flee before it to the Loire. I hunt for a place to land and let it pass.

A clearing. I cut the throttle. A few bumps. I land without flipping over. An instant later the snow catches up with me and I find myself in obscurity. Nose in my cockpit, dripping, I submit to the squall for a quarter of an hour, and when it passes, my Spad, the plowed field, the forest of Compiègne, all of the countryside is white and I am frozen.

It took me half an hour to find some resting artillerymen in a small village, who sheltered, warmed, and restored me and loaned me a horse. I trotted to a squadron not too far off toward Pierrefonds. I brought back a tractor and two mechanics to refuel and put my Spad, which two telegraphers were guarding, back in flying condition.

After six hours' absence, I returned to the field. Piston, more familiar with the single-seater than I, had disengaged himself from the snow cloud (which he perhaps found less thick) and was able, with some difficulty it is true, to return to the squadron, where they were quite concerned about me.


. . . March. "You won't be allowed to leave again without me, Lieutenant. Bad things happen to you when I don't watch you."

"Well! and you? Was it confetti you got in your wings over Soissons? Anyhow, if you don't want to let me go alone, get your plane out of its stall, because, as for me, I am warming my engine."

Actually my Spad is idling to raise the water temperature in the radiator. Flying suit, stocking,* headgear, goggles. Take off. Chelcher follows.

*See note, p. 185.

Stand-off

What a machine the single-seater is for one who comes from a Farman! The Nieuport is lighter, flies by itself; the Spad is heavier and with it, one must not stunt imprudently close to the ground, but what a wonderful crate—balance, speed, smoothness . . . In piloting it, one feels as if he had wings on his arms. I begin to feel comfortable in my taxi; a good tight seat, a machine gun, almost no instruments; a clock, an altimeter, a map the size of your hand; and to fly, almost no movement, rather a touch of the finger. It might be said that the plane obeys the force of my will alone.

For three quarters of an hour we see nothing but an R.4 taking photos in the midst of German shell bursts. We find ourselves at about 12,000 feet over the Oise, down stream from Chauny.

Two planes in front of us. The first almost at our altitude, the other lower. The closest is a two-seater, green camouflage, with large wings and small fuselage which seems too slender.

I don't think that they have seen us. I dive like lead. He draws near. I see his black crosses bordered in white grow larger. He has a number on the side of his fuselage. He must be close enough for me to start firing on him. I get him in my sights and I start to fire, tac, tac, tac. My taxi drops very rapidly. There is wind in my eyes, I feel myself projected above my top wing. The Boche grows bigger and bigger. After all, I don't want to fly into him. I hit the stick. I climb some distance by the speed I have gained. For an instant I lose sight of the Boche who did not want to fall. In his surprise he has not fired on me.

Chelcher attacks in his turn. The Boche dives. My comrade fires at point blank, makes a "to the left" in order not to rush into him and starts over again from behind and from above. The Boche replies uninterruptedly. After 3000 feet of whirlwind descent, Chelcher breaks off the combat and climbs toward me.

I wonder if I should attack again also, but the second Boche comes back, followed by another more rapid, who comes from the east. My comrade goes off toward our lines. I follow without insisting on a fight which becomes too unequal. Chelcher goes straight to the south, passing the trenches, reaches the field, lands and I behind him.

Again his machine is hit everywhere. His upper right wing has to be changed, his aileron controls are half cut through.

"A pretty roughing up you got," says Bertrand, "but we will end by picking you up in pieces. You are wrecking a Spad a day. After all, I can't send you to Bourget every morning."

# III

"After a heavy artillery preparation, our troops attacking German trenches, found them unoccupied. We continue to move toward the north and our advanced troops have reached Noyon . . ."
(Official Army Communique)

The Boches have gone! These trenches which have stopped us since September 1914 are empty. Our troops at last advance and for the first time with a free field before them, after having been so long stalemated.

For us the surprise was less striking than for the

rear. The fires throughout the region forewarned us of the retreat; the enemy could not devastate the countryside so completely without intending to abandon it. On the other hand, the Germans have evaded the attack which we were preparing. We are slightly discountenanced, like a boxer whose fist hits empty air.

But the event retains all of its immense importance. We have reconquered a part of the invaded country, the Boches have gone! Has this which we so much desired been realized so quickly? Up to now, the most stubborn efforts have failed to push the line back more than fifteen kilometers; today the plain is free to the horizon.

But what ruin we find! I don't think the Germans have ever showed so senseless a violence in destruction, so obvious a desire to destroy for the sole pleasure of destroying. The sacking of the Department of the Oise will remain, I am sure, one of their great crimes. We begin to dream of future reprisals.

In single-seaters, we fly down the Aisne, then we fly up the Oise. Here are lines over which we can fly at hedge hopping level; here are gun emplacements. The artillery squadrons are going to have an unmixed pleasure in visiting these places so long inaccessible and in verifying the accuracy of their photo interpretations. This visit, incidentally, will not be without danger. We are warned that the Boches have left booby traps in shelters and trenches—exploding doors, cans of bully beef, packs of tobacco loaded with cheddite, etc.

Beyond the lines, the forest of Laigle. The beautiful chateaus à la française which decorate it have been devastated—caved-in wings, gaping facades, roofs fallen in. Some are razed within six feet of the ground; others have only their four walls, empty shells without floors or partitions, through whose gaping holes of windows daylight passes. Near the chateaus, the villages destroyed by dynamite and set afire are still smoking. Church, town hall, houses and barns have been thoroughly demolished down to shoulder height; some seen from above leave nothing on the ground but a black trace of burnt and scattered straw.

The devastation is so complete and so perfect that it makes one think rather of a natural cataclysm, an earthquake or a cyclone than of man's work.

The fruit trees are cut to the ground as are the trees along the torn-up roads full of gaping holes; the large poplars felled in the water on the sunken barges block the bed of the canal. All along the Oise, the railroad track is torn up.

And that goes as far as Ham, as far as Saint-Simon, as far as Chauny and Tergnier. Nothing has been spared except Noyon. Noyon is still standing and its streets are full of inhabitants who run to meet our soldiers. The cavalry, spahis in khaki with red saddles pass beyond the town and press on to all the surrounding points. Our infantry is a bit hesitant. After twenty-seven months in the trenches it feels strange in the open country and marches with cautious steps, fearing an ambush or a machine gun behind every clump of trees.

We circle over Noyon at 600 feet, for the clouds are low. The cathedral square swarms like an ant hill. A regimental band is playing to celebrate our return. We can distinguish the concentric circles;

the public, the notables, the musicians and band leader in the center.

I make a vertical dive on the crowd to do it the honor of a little exhibition. But my idea is a failure; my plane is taken for a Boche and in an instant the square is empty. I am sorry not to have seen the band leader closer, the trombone player and the big bass drum galloping for shelter.

During this time Bertrand lands on the parade ground at Noyon and informs the infantrymen that they have nothing in front of them and that they can advance.

We return, cutting across from Noyon toward Fontenoy, a deserted and flooded zone which has not yet been occupied, where the beautiful beeches of the forest stand sadly, their feet in the water.

. . . March. Weather of seasonal change which mingles countless white clouds with the blue of the sky. We climb in this labyrinth of fleece, to carry out our patrol, adjutant Cavel, Costard nicknamed Coco, a youth who pilots a Nieuport, and I.

We see the ground only intermittently through tunnels of dazzling white cloud which open and close. Cavel, who has a love of acrobatics and a gift for it, at times dives through a dense patch of fleecy cloud and comes out 600 feet below. The Spad, narrow spindle, speeds through the air like an aerial torpedo.

Twelve thousand. The air becomes icy, near zero; we are still in the clouds. Suddenly, I hear the clatter of a machine gun. Cavel in this labyrinth has fallen unexpectedly on a Boche on whom he fires point blank.

[161]

The Boche side slips and disappears, probably shot down. But who can inform us of the fall which no one has been able to see from the ground with this overcast sky?

At 13,500 we finally are above the fleece. Below us a snowy-white field with holes here and there showing the ground. Solitude. All three of us sway in pure and icy space. My hands, my body and my feet, heated by the motor, do not suffer too much, but my face puckers with cold, my mouth is chapped under the hoar frost of my moustache, my frozen nose hurts me. The thermometer of my Spad goes down to 50 degrees and does not want to rise. What will I do if I have to dive? Fourteen thousand five hundred. Towards Saint-Quentin, a somber silhouette skims a sea of clouds, followed by its shadow hopping at its side.

A Boche!—Cavel dives. I follow him, while Coco, a novice, does not understand the maneuver and remains above.

The Boche, who suspects nothing, receives my comrade right on his head, panics, dives frantically, tries to turn and does not succeed in shaking off Cavel, who empties his whole belt in his rear.

I follow the chase, but my temperature begins to go down. Diving in this bitter cold my radiator freezes and I am surely going to stall my prop. I leave Cavel and hit the throttle. A few sputters. The Hispano takes hold with coaxing, but takes hold. Beneath me the two combatants disappear into a hole, the one always following the other.

Coco is lost to view. I do not insist on finding him and continue my patrol alone. I fly again down the Ailette. Not a crate on the horizon.

Two flashes of light attract my attention. They are two planes which from the distance seem almost transparent. I would not have seen them if they had not, in turning, caught the sun. They are a bit above me, on the right.

There are days when one feels brave. I pull on the stick to reach them. They are two single-seaters; one of them, heavy, with a large short muzzle, with black crosses lost in the camouflage of somber green, has the air of a crudely built Spad; the other with its protruding pointed ailerons similar to those of the Taubes of another time, with clean bright wings as if made of thin metal, a tail in comma form, a light grey belly, well designated dirty little crosses.

I am 900 feet below the second. I do a chandelle* and I fire. A few shots—I am jammed. A lousy tool.

It's the Boche's turn; he maneuvers with decision, he dives and I see his prop turning over slowly, a bright disc; his machine gun spits and phosphorous bullets pass, making a white trail like a serpentine at the fair.

I feel myself in a bad position. I hit the rudder bar. I get out of the cone of fire and run for home. The Boches remain up there and I have the vexed feeling that they have just thrown me off a balcony. Luckily they do not pursue me, for I cannot dive indefinitely with this falling temperature, and my motor about to freeze up.

Out of reach, I fight with my Vickers, which refuses to function. I have nothing to do but go home. I take twenty minutes to lose altitude, not daring to dive, with my thermometer below 40 and constantly fearing that I will kill my motor.

Coco has already landed. Cavel arrives in turn. He lost his second Boche in a cloud, like the first, and rails against the infantry observers who did not see his encounters.

*A "zoom," or sudden steep climb.

. . . March. Piston lands in his Nieuport 110 followed by Coco, his faithful shadow. He rushes up to Bertrand.

"I got that one, Lieutenant. I got him. Have to get it confirmed. His wing started to flame and smoke. A large yellow one, Lieutenant. As a matter of fact, I had brought some Buckinghams.* Coco saw it all. Did you see it, Coco? You see! I dived, he dived; I dived all out. I fired two hundred rounds. My machine gun is terrific, Lieutenant. I only have to breathe on it for it to fire. When I saw the wing hit, I corrected my fire on his center and he fell in the forest. A big yellow one, Lieutenant. Have to get it confirmed."

"It will be the easier since you give me plenty of details . . ."

That evening Headquarters telephones us that a German plane was indeed brought down near Coucy and it was going to be credited to Piston.

"That," says the captain of the air service who was speaking, "is your last victory in the Aisne. The army is going to get a rest. As for you, we are lending you as reinforcement to a pursuit group which is forming in Champagne. You will doubtless be leaving in a few days."

Thanks anyhow.


. . . 27 March. This evening we went to Noyon, the boss and I, to take our final orders from the army which we are leaving. A drive under the loveliest storm which March can offer us. Wind,

---

*Buckinghams. A type of bullet used for shooting down balloons. J. B. V. Some account of this ammunition will be found in *War Birds: Diary of an Unknown Aviator*, N.Y., George H. Doran (© 1926), pp. 239-40.

snow, rain, and squalls of sleet. The ride of the Valkyries in a Pan-Pan* 24 hp.

At the old lines, at Ribécourt, our troubles begin. The Germans have torn up two kilometers of paving, destroyed the railroad, choked the canal. The engineers have built a road of tree trunks where only one vehicle at a time can pass. Over this single-lane road defiles all day, and night too, artillery, troops, materiel, supplies, etc. For twenty minutes we see large trucks pass, skidding in the mud, close together, bottled up, whipped by the rain. We are under the care of a reservist dripping with water, his hood raised, his rifle at port. Under the gusts to relieve our impatience, he takes us to see the old defenses, the listening posts, the network of barbed wire.

It is our turn to run the bottle neck. A special man, who rides back and forth at the head of each convoy, sits down in the seat of our light car.

From a shapeless mass of wet and shining raincoats comes a voice with an Oxford accent, which says to our chauffeur:

"A real Walpurgis night."

"I don't know," answers this simple man, "but it is devilishly slippery and my rear axle is getting knocked off on these damn timbers."

This night is really too romantic. The wind shakes the car top as if to tear it off, the melted snow comes through chinks of the canvas and wets us under our covers.

Noyon. In the darkness the town is a maze; we wander about looking for the cathedral, a point of reference which will direct us to headquarters. Complete night. Our headlights light German

---

*Pan-Pan, that is, a Panhard, a make of car.

signs in gothic black on white—"Wechsel," "Metzger," etc., which give the town a foreign air.

At the Army, where we finally find the offices, the order of yesterday is confirmed. The 705 is sent urgently to Champagne. We have to pack our baggage, send our rolling stock at the double, leave the first day of good weather.

"Besides they have complimented us," adds Bertrand as we get into the car. "They find that the squadron has done good work during the advance and has deserved well of the _____th army."

"*Non Gloria Nobis Sed Tibi Domine.* You have marched in front and the cortege has followed. It is in the scope of the most modest courage."

"Do me the favor not to kid me with your foreign languages. All that doesn't keep us from going to lend support to a big job in a dirty sector after a winter of hard work."

"Obviously."

An identical return journey in intense cold on crowded roads.

# IV

*Camp de la Monnette. Champagne.*

. . . 30 March 1917. When we arrived at the group, we were very cordially welcomed.

"You come at a good time," we were told. "There were not enough of us and we had to fly six hours a day. Beefed up by a squadron we will perhaps fly only four, when the sector is quiet."

"And the Boches?"

"The Boches? Don't worry, they are not lacking here, and with aces. Unfortunately, Baldamus* was killed at a dog fight around the balloons yesterday, but his friends remain. You will only have to go over the lines to chat with them . . ."

In downpours (why does it always have to rain each time I change fields?) we watch our tents being put up in the little pine grove. This evening, in the heather "still wet with rain," our folding cots will be installed. When we sit down at the top of the cot to go to bed, it will flip over and scatter our bedding all over the ground. If we manage to get under covers, our dirty feet will carry into bed mud, blades of grass, bits of rotten wood which when we wake tomorrow will make a heavy leaf mold.

After a while everything more or less settles down, fairly smoothly, into calm, and thanks to the kindness of the neighboring units.

At Camp de la Monnette we are four squadrons which form the pursuit group, the G.C. 42. Four squadrons of single-seaters, Nieuports and Spads. Especially Spads, whose role in Champagne, where they say we must attack, is to assure the security of the sector and to protect the planes of the Army Corps in making the life of the Boches as insupportable as possible.

Our mission thus is uniquely combat. The group assures a squadron of single-seaters permanently over the lines.

The squadron on duty is divided in three patrols echeloned at different heights, patrols of three or four planes which must fly for two hours on a designated front.

*Baldamus, a German ace. J. B. V.

Before this squadron has left the lines, another replaces it. Thus we do two patrols of two hours each daily in good weather.

Under our protection, the spotting, liaison, and photo planes quietly do their modest task. While protecting these less well armed brothers, we try to corner a Boche and if we fail to bring him down, we at least force him to give way and run for home.

Nevertheless, it must be said that in this large sector a Boche sometimes slips through our fingers, waits until we have our backs turned to jump on an innocent Farman (for at the dawn of the fourth summer, Farmans are still seen over the lines), or to take a photo of the trench and return in machine gunning our infantrymen. But these escapades are rare; when the patrol appears, the Boches flee for home and our presence leaves the sky clear.

The great leader of the group is Major Hermant.* It is unnecessary to talk of his reputation and his service record. He is a real chief and a real war flier; physically a bit heavy, calm, whom no one can bluff, benevolent, actively courageous and quietly energetic.

I am deeply grateful to him for having been one I could esteem, love and admire. Men of his value are not found everywhere. Now, such men are needed to command pursuit aviation, a choice arm which can be given only to the best leaders. The army and bombardment corps have first rate people, but nowhere in aviation is there so diffi-

*Major Brocard, a great soldier, shot down in enemy territory in 1915, escaped and later brilliantly commanded a pursuit group. J. B. V. Some account of Major Félix Brocard's career may be found in Aaron Norman's *The Great Air War* (Macmillan, 1968).

*Kyrie Eleison*

cult and constant an effort to be made, a way of fighting so dangerous and exhausting, losses so great, a morale as spirited and high as in the fighter squadrons.

We have made acquaintance with the pilots of the group, who have filled us in on the sector where we start to work tomorrow.

Last Monday, they had a great show, with a romp together against the Boche, while the volunteers attacked the barrage balloons; it is an operation which consists of diving behind the balloon whose winch winds it down rapidly, and trying to set it afire with incendiary bullets. Sometimes it is necessary to pursue it down to 600 feet during which time you are drawing fire from machine guns and anti-aircraft. No one knows how the volunteers, who were on pins and needles, passed the night before the balloon party.

Still, the group knocked down two of the goat skins. Furthermore, a young pilot, who did not have twenty hours of flying over the lines, in returning from having missed his balloon, had to fight a Boche. During the combat he collided and hit the upper wing of his adversary with his right wheel. The Nieuport came back undamaged, but the Boche crashed. It is believed to be Baldamus, the ace of Champagne.

. . . 31 March. Patrol this morning in company of the chief and Loris. The weather is half good and half bad, very fair in the east but the sky in the west covered by a bank of clouds. In vain we hurry from Tahure to Reims and from Reims to Prosnes attracted by the white shell bursts indicating the Boches, but each time the Fritz have disappeared when we arrive.

Toward nine o'clock, a Spad, quite some distance from us, at 12,000 over the Montagne de Reims,* attacks a two-seater which is returning from an unknown sally over our lines. When the Frenchman lets go of the Boche we try to get to him in our turn, but he flees like the devil, and before we can get near him, he has plunged into the layer of fog and slipped back to his own lines.

It is bizarre weather this afternoon. At 3500 feet a layer of scattered clouds; above, a magnificent sky.

The squadron could only send seven Spads over the lines—a patrol of four, between 10,500 and 12,000, another three at 6000 to protect the spotter planes.

For this lower patrol, which I command, the situation is complicated; if we fly under the clouds at 3000 or 3300, the Boches will pass above the ceiling without our being able to do anything. If we fly at 6000, they will hide under the clouds and being neither seen nor known, will do their little reconnaissance.

What we anticipated takes place; all of a sudden we see three green planes, which after having flown over our lines—how many times we don't know—fly for home full speed, in single file. We see they are flying full out, for their tail fins are higher than their noses 'and puffs of smoke are coming out of their exhaust pipes. The whole patrol goes for the Fritz; like arrows we go through a cloud, coming out of which Sagny just misses hitting me. I pursue a camouflaged two-seater; large wings, large stabilizer, and a very little fuselage, which is too thin, marked with white numbers.

*Montagne de Reims, a height southwest of the city.

Target Destroyed

I fire on him, he fires on me. The puffs of his explosive shells look like toy balloons from the Louvre*, but I have to give him up at 1500 or 1800 feet over Beine and my return is accompanied by machine gun bursts from the ground. But a Spad flies fast . . .

The infantrymen who saw these crates disporting themselves over their heads will say that we are bunglers and good for nothings and that we intentionally allow enemy planes to fly over the sector. How they would scream if they saw as do the Germans, enemy patrols constantly flying three kilometers behind their lines, for we are scarcely ever over our lines during the two hours which our forays last, flying almost entirely in enemy territory, despite the severe anti-aircraft fire they inflict on us.


. . . April. High patrol, with Chelcher and Legrand.

At nine thousand we see a patrol of five planes, which fly a bit above us in the direction of the enemy. I imagine they are comrades whom we should relieve, and vexed at going less far in the lines than they, I try to approach them. But they withdraw before us, continuing to gain altitude. I understand my error; it was the Boches to whom I was going to pay my respects.

I recognize them now: five single-seaters, Albatroses; they climb at the same time as we and warily look us over. Without attacking they allow us to encroach several kilometers over their territory. They have several hundred feet advantage in

*Toy balloons were given to children by the Louvre, a large department store near the museum.

altitude over us and will not let us get near them. It irritates me to be dominated by those taxis.

At fifteen thousand feet the two patrols continue to look each other over, we below. At 15,500 we give up the constant climbing; this could continue indefinitely and the Spads are laboring seriously. And then, it is cold; my nose is curling up and my lips are chapping; I have the feeling that my face is shrinking, shrinking. We thus stay between 14,500 and 15,000, watching and being watched without seeing anyone else over the sector except our five comrades.

A little before the end of the foray, we dive on a two-seater which passes over the lines near Prosnes; but scarcely do we make a movement when the Albatroses start to come down on our heads and we are obliged to face them, leaving the other Boche to go home. One can't court trouble far in enemy lines with the threat of so unequal a fight.

On landing, I ascertain that I have a frozen face, my nose is burned like a triple sunburn and when I take off my glasses the skin comes off with their circle of rubber. My comrades say that the frost bite does not look good on me; in any case it hurts me.

Legrand, who was so imprudent as to take off his glove to fiddle with his pressure pump, has his thumb and index finger on the left hand frozen. He has large blisters on his skin as if burned with hot water. His whole arm is swollen; he suffers and he will not be able to fly for a week or two.


. . . April. There are too many mechanics who in a poetic vein compare the pursuit plane to a vulture stalking its prey. Why not an eagle or even a roc of the *Arabian Nights*?

Moreover the comparison is only half right; one or two machines alone, very high, hovering in the air and watching for a victim may present a predatory appearance. But the victim has a double cutting edge so to speak; the partridge or the rabbit has defenses, namely, a machine gun, sometimes two, whose bullets, if they are not explosive, are incendiary.

But what an exciting fight! Over our lines or a little over those of the enemy, the single-seater stays hidden in the sun so that, blinded, the planes cannot see him from below. He waits.

Six thousand feet below, the game arrives, suspecting nothing; the observer works his transmitter, shoots his pictures or passes the time of day. The hunter settles himself in his seat, takes a breath, cuts his engine and falls like a stone on the back of the Boche.

If the Fritz has seen nothing, the first attack is not too dangerous and one can risk firing on the enemy from above. One starts to fire as close as possible to the target and stops only to pull up to avert a collision. Then, as the German observer has jumped for his machine gun, to attack again one must get out of the field of fire, that is to say, below the enemy plane, to protect himself by the German's own fuselage; a maneuver which, with an alert adversary, is less easy to perform than to talk about.

There are three kinds of pilots: those who have to be coaxed to get past the balloons and never attack a Boche at less than 1200 feet. One must hurry to give these fellows their Croix de Guerre, the desire of which is the only thing that keeps them at the front and which various big shots discreetly claim for them twice a month; and send them without delay to a service in the rear more in conformity with their aptitudes.

Then there are the aces, the great aces. They are people apart, who join courage with a special gift. Their decisiveness, their speed, their precision, their address put them as far from us common pilots as a Chinese juggler from a good tennis player. I remember finding myself at the same time as P . . . above a Boche. I asked myself how I was going to attack him. Abruptly, I saw P . . . who, an instant earlier, was beside me, firing from a hundred feet at the tail of the Fritz, who started to burn. I am still astounded by the way the thing was done. Such aces should attack with only the minimum of risk and the maximum chance of knocking down their adversary. They must avoid exposing themselves unnecessarily; their services are too valuable!

Nothing is similar to the situation of the third kind of pilots, good group fliers.

These, trained and skillful, do not have the mastery of the preceding; when they take on a plane, they have a good chance of missing, for firing with a fixed machine gun is extremely difficult. But if they do not shoot down a Boche, they interfere with his work and force him to reenter his lines. They are the watch dogs. To these pilots go the heavy work, the screening, the protection. It is enough for them to be energetic and courageous and to attack all enemy planes who try to fly over our trenches. It is among these I ask permission to put myself, as do the majority of those around me; we are not aces, but we do a useful work. Plenty of enemy two-seaters, because of us, have been obliged to abandon their mission, or

Accidental Victory

bring back their observer killed or wounded. One day or another, an enemy will surely go down, if one of us does not precede him . . . For the pitcher that goes too often to the well . . .

Our patrol lasts two hours, hours during which it is not only a question of hunting for the Boche, but also of watching continually not to be surprised by another hunter. Stalkers, we are stalked. The aggressor can come from all directions. A hand held up to the sun which blinds us, our eyes blinking, we look toward this light which can hide a single-seater, above and invisible, or else, twisting our necks, we look behind us or under the dead spot of our wing, which hides the ground.

In this tension, this desire to surprise, this fear of being surprised, in the cold, the altitude, the lack of oxygen,* one hundred and twenty minutes of flight are exhausting. If we dive so much as only two or three times from 15,000 to 6,000 feet on a Boche who turns out to be a Salmson-Moineau,** we feel our eyes stick out like those of a lobster and our stomachs come up into our mouths and beyond. Only the idea of a Fritz whom we hope to encounter and bring down shortens these moments. The hours are shortened by fights during which all other preoccupation disappears. The pursuit makes us forget fatigue and the danger of the chase.

Nevertheless, a great effort is needed to get into one's taxi and to leave again, when one has already flown during the morning, when one is sleepy, feels his arms and legs heavy, has an empty head, and the smell of the hot motors makes him queazy.

*We did not have oxygen masks. J. B. V.
**An obsolete French plane, still flying in 1917. J. B. V.

Three pilots who are less stiff and tired fly the high patrol at twelve or fifteen thousand feet. The others fly at 10,500 or 6,000. All, moreover, encounter Boches. There are some at all different altitudes and we fight every day at 15,000, or 3,000, sometimes with an Albatros who scrapes the ceiling, sometimes with a low flying plane which is infantry spotting.

This morning a Boche tried to fly over the lines at 14,000 at the eastern extremity of the sector. We attacked him when he was four kilometers within our lines and pushing for home as hard as he could.

Chelcher fired on him first, then Piston, then I, and all three without result. Still we got as close to him as we could. I saw the machine gunner in his turret as I see you, the insignia on the side of the fuselage and the face of the pilot.

As the Boche was going home after having taken our triple salvo, a Spad of the N.840 which came to relieve us, got under his tail and fired a band of incendiary shells at him. The poor Fritz started to spin and crashed over the trenches in the midst of shell holes.

At the same time the lower patrol had a lively engagement with two Boches who tried to fly over the lines at about 3000 feet, to do I know not what behind our lines.

"Big crates," said Sagny, "with fuselages as big as that, in plywood. They fired on us with a double-barrelled machine gun which made a terrible row. On seeing the patrol, a single-seater, which accompanied them, coolly left them. If they had not been so low we would have had all of them, but they got home and after all we could not run behind their stabilizers at ground level as far as Pont-Faverger."

# V

Bertrand and I are taking a walk under the two Bessonneaus which are big enough to hold our twelve single-seaters, not very bulky playthings. The mechanics work around the Spads, taking them apart, adjusting and cleaning, and of Octave, buried in a fuselage, can be seen only his feet, which stick out of the place generally occupied by the head of the pilot.

Bertrand says to me:

"What allows us to hold up in these days of intense activity, and to put enough planes over the lines every morning is that we have splendid mechanics, who are as devoted and skillful as possible.

"I don't know why aviation mechanics have the reputations of loafers; nothing is more unjust. Their only fault is that they are a bit unruly and tend to be blowhards, but aside from that they are good fellows from whom we can get some marvelous work.

"Of course, we must not ask them to have their blue coveralls pressed the night before, to spring to attention, and to address us in the third person, like a butler. But when they have the respect of their pilot and pride in their plane, they will knock out a tremendous lot of work and will not hesitate to work all night so that their crate will always be in shape.

"Fancy the expression of a senior mechanic whose pilot would say to him: 'I don't trust you anymore.' The other day, my two good fellows took the cowl off my Spad, changed the radiator and put back the cowl in twenty-four hours, and you know, with all of the screws which hold the sheet metal of our crates, it is no little thing. Our mechanics, at two per plane, have a good six or eight hours of work a day just to keep it up, and this is not to mention the days of big repairs. The Hispano is a delicate motor and, mounted on a Spad, it is hard to get at; the slightest damage demands a day's work, whereas the Nieuports, with their rotary engine, can be taken down and put together in no time at all.

"Really, I ask myself how an escadrille can make out if it does not have a good personnel; what would we do without our crew of mechanics who know the ropes, whom nothing bothers, and who have a feeling for motors like others for horses or for piloting."

Sitting on a can of gasoline, Sabot, Chelcher's mechanic, sticks out his tongue, a paint brush in his hand. He has become the artist decorator and paints on the fuselage of the Spad the red comet, insigne of the escadrille.

For each squadron has its individual emblem—a stork, an eagle, a duck, a dragon, a cross of Lorraine, the head of an American Sioux,* a hand of Fatima,** a tiger, a rose, or the sun, depending on the heroic, playful, or lyric whim of those who have chosen it.

In addition, each pilot has his personal mono-

---

*An Indian's head was an insigne of the Lafayette Escadrille, manned by American pilots. J. B. V.

**Fatima was the daughter of Mahomet. The hand of Fatima is often found on Islamic monuments, and some Moslems carry it as an amulet. Certain authorities maintain that this emblem even ante-dates Islam and that it was venerated by pre-Islamic Semites.

The escadrilles of the Army Corps recruited in North Africa (Algeria, Tunis, Morocco) had chosen this emblem, many of the "Khaki" soldiers being Moslems. J. B. V.

gram which more or less discreetly decorates his plane, a number or fetish which, despite regulations, he has substituted for a simple number which alone should identify his plane. Navarre had a tri-color Nieuport. P . . . a black Spad, M . . . a blood-red plane, and the value which we place on those individual markings which accompany us in our flights and in our combats shows that fliers are no less superstitious than sailors. Witness the touch-wood, and the silk stocking with which we bind our heads under the fur helmet—a trophy* without which those pilots I knew would not want to fly.

We wander under the hangars, looking over the work of the mechanics, the fitters, the gunsmiths, all the material life of the escadrille. I think that we are the only ones up; the other pilots, who put all worry aside on getting out of their planes, sleep on their beds waiting the hour of duty. The altitude, the tension, the fatigue have given all of us a kind of perpetual stoop and sleeping sickness; outside of patrol hours, scarcely taking time to eat, we sleep, with wooly mouths and buzzing head.

"Let's go! I'm going to sign some papers," says Bertrand.

"Wait a minute, here come some crates hedge hopping which are going to land; they must be the 721st which was announced for today and which is coming to reinforce the groups."

Seven or eight Spads circle at a hundred feet over the field, looking for the landing direction.

Suddenly one of them which banks over the

---

*In the French, *dépouille opime*, a rich spoil. The flier who carried away a woman's stocking as a trophy, would tie it around his head before going on a flight, as described.

pine woods, nose dives, spins and buries itself in the ground at full speed, the motor first.

Impossible to know what happened; the foot of the pilot suddenly slipped, one of his controls stuck, or he turned too sharply for his speed. In any case the plane got away from him so rapidly that he did not have time to correct it.

A dead man whom they carry out with head wobbling.

It is ten minutes to one. The gathering around the wrecked Spad is already dispersed. Cavel comes out of the tent, stretches, then de Loris with his eyes swollen, Chelcher who still has a stomach ache from a hurried lunch. The other pilots.

The Spads, in line, face the wind, motors turning over slowly to warm up, while we get dressed.

"I'm fed up, Lieutenant," declares Sagny.

"What can I do, old man? Do you think anyone around here is very lively? Hurry up, we are going to take off five minutes late, as we did yesterday."

And Chelcher:

"If I could only knock down one of those dirty Fritz, I would sleep all day and all night and try not to think of a crate for twenty-four hours."

"You know very well that P . . . doesn't leave any Boches for his little friends; he knocks down one a day in pieces or in flames. Again yesterday he polished off a two-seater over Prosnes; the crate broke up in the air. How does he do it, the lucky dog? As for me, I attack the Fritz, at close range in vain; they are as well off as I am after the fight."

"P . . . himself told me that he got his first one only after at least forty dog fights . . ."

The pilots climb into their cockpits, buckle their straps.

"Chelcher, with your straps and leather helmet, you look like that Boche in a single-seater who fled before us the other day, turning from time to time and hitting his rudder bar to keep out of our line of fire."

"One more we could have plucked and which we muffed . . . well, at 3000 over La Cheppe?"

"Right."

At 10,500, Chelcher on my right, de Loris on my left, we hover over Boche territory via Auberive, Moronvilliers, Beine.

Near Pont-Faverger, two dark spots pass over the Suippe. The two-seaters approach and make a big swing toward the west, slow, prudent, hesitant. We return toward our lines so that the fire of the mobile guns does not reveal our presence. The Boches arrive; they are one behind the other at 7500.

I dive on the first; he looms larger, he is very near. Who can describe how it feels to be so close to an enemy? We are the only ones, with the infantrymen, who really see him, strike him directly, know anger, agony, the shifting chances of single combat. The appearance of the black crosses, the two men in the cockpit, overwhelms me and I lose a bit of command of myself. I aim, I fire, I can follow my tracer bullets, which frame the Boche. He does a sharp left and dives to get away. I feel his surprise, his panic, his fear. I turn with him and I fire again, then in order not to ram him, I turn aside and let him go.

Already Chelcher is on him. I see the bullets leave his machine gun; the Boche answers and does a vertical spiral; his heavy motor helps him descend rapidly. He has drawn us several kilometers into his territory and is only at 3500 feet. We abandon him.

I look toward de Loris who no longer fires; his Boche dives straight down; smoke is coming from his fuselage, he starts to spin and we see him crash to the ground. I hope it will be confirmed, but all of these combats take place behind enemy lines and it is difficult to find witnesses.

We return by Auberive under heavy ground fire, and here near de Prunay are white bursts from French guns. I fly rapidly toward them, even too rapidly, for my two companions do not see me leave and I find myself alone.

At 3500, over the lines, where they pass to the south of the Roman road, a large Boche plane. He must be infantry spotting, for a red pennant floats from one of his struts.

I go to meet him, trying to bar the route to the north, but he has seen me and dives for home while his machine gunner fires explosive bullets at me, leaving white puffs.

I pursue him also firing, furious against this big crate which I attack from such short range and which refuses to fall. The ground comes up terribly fast. I look at my altimeter, it shows 1500 feet. Our trenches are already a long way off. I cannot expose myself any farther and I put on the gas to return home.

Putt!—Putt!—sputters! My motor does not catch; if I pull up the stick, my prop is going to stall. I quickly slow down. I look at the temperature, it is at twenty-five degrees; in the prolonged dive the water got cold and as for the pressure it has fallen almost to zero.

My stick between my knees to have my hands

free, I pump up the pressure of the tank and fiddle with the gas lever.

Putt—Putt—the sputterings continue. A forced landing behind enemy lines!

The Spad goes down and down; these machines do not glide much; the altimeter unwinds—900 feet. I distinctly see the pines as they go by, shell holes, the details on the ground. And here is a regular tac tac, which is not that of the disappeared Boche, but the firing of machine guns on the ground for which I am certainly a pretty target. And then several cannon shots very close make me jump in my seat.

My motor catches a bit. I don't dare put on full throttle. I have 700 rpm, 750 feet.

There is a green place between the lines, in the neutral zone, where few shells fall. I recall having noticed this corner thrusting toward the north. If I could get there, flip over in the barbed wire and reach the French trenches on foot?

A bullet passes through the tip of my right wing. I see the insignificant hole which it leaves, a mere pin-prick in the canvas. I bend all my will on my little green corner. The ground machine gun follows me and I look in the sky to see if, to complete my misfortune a plane is not falling on my back. Less than 600 feet.

The mis-firings diminish; 750, 800 rpm, the motor is turning over, and I am out of the mess. I put on full power, my motor purrs happily, I climb with all my might, my mind flooded with relief. I fly over the lines, I am among my own and I regain altitude to rejoin my comrades.

The Spads land one by one. They roll heavily towards the hangars, gunning the motor, scraping the ground with their tail skids. The mechanics run and grasp the ends of the wings. The first pilot to arrive stops, unbuckles, takes off his goggles, lifts himself from his seat and sits on the edge of the cockpit. He cries: "Did you see the Boche?" "Did I see him, and how!" "And the big one I dived on?" "The red brown who fired incendiaries." "Did you see me fight with the three single-seaters who were lurking over Tahure?" "I fired on him from below." "I fired on him point blank—chandelle—wing over . . . a jerk at the stick . . . a jamming. I have a shell in my wing." "One in my fuselage." "The Albatros . . . , the two-seater . . .", etc.

The pilots talk, talk. They all have something special to relate; they are chattering, edgy. The more reserved hold long discourses with their comrades, with the mechanics, with strangers, idlers, off-duty infantrymen, or artillerymen, gathered to listen.

After two hours of mental tension, of lurking for prey, of combats, of solitude, of mental oppression and of cold, they go in a few minutes from 12,000 feet to the ground and, drunk with oxygen, with burning eyes, buzzing heads, numbed arms and legs, they relax in broken chatter, nervous and incoherent.

Little Bergamot of the 740 lands and says nothing. He cuts his motor, comes in too high, makes a rough landing, and his Spad comes to rest across the field.

From the distance we see his head resting on the cockpit edge, his face so pale that we run to him in haste.

He has his hand on his stomach which a bullet has pierced and the fur of his glove is sticky with blood.

His face is wrinkled like that of an old man, his eyes are astonished and wild. Still he has a pale smile when we get to him.

From Nauroy, where he was wounded, it took all of his will power to return to the field and now he does not have the strength to talk.

Gently we take him by the shoulders from the bloody seat. We lay him on the ground while waiting a stretcher. We have to keep off his dog, which uneasy, comes to put his cold nose on his face.

We carry him off.

# VI

If I were not so tired and dazed by the hours of flight at 13,500 or 14,000 feet, I would like to write a book on what I know of my profession, on what I see and hear around me.

For this book, I have already found a title: *Annals of a Pursuit Group.* Only, to be in the atmosphere to write it, I would not shut myself up in my room in front of a sheet of paper. I would install myself in the midst of my comrades, at the corner of a table in the bar of our group.

There I would be in the atmosphere—gay, carefree, and dashing. I would feel myself with my friends and my peers. I would listen to the talk full of useful information and strong images.

A captain would shake poker dice with a second lieutenant for his glass of port.

"We're even—a sharp throw—three kings; your turn, Captain."

Or else, interminably, "no trump."

Or again: "Attack three quarters in front—a chandelle to jump the Boche from above, then a sharp bank to put yourself under his tail."

"His plane suddenly rose. I thought it was to break off, but no, the pilot was hit and the plane started to spin right to the ground."

"We had been telling him for several days, 'you're pushing too hard,' but he wouldn't listen and we couldn't hold him. He got a bullet in his head in boring in on a two-seater."

And the phonograph, indifferent to it all, would sing, "Hello! hello! where's your lady friend?" as if we could know things like that.

I would tell about our existence. But for those who do not live it with us, isn't this dull? Is it very thrilling to read, "Patrol over Beine. Patrol over Nauroy. Patrol over the Suippe. Combat, combat and still more combat; and every day, so and so, and two pilots of such and such an outfit —and still others—have been killed on the field, have fallen in flames, or have not returned."

That is all that my book would say. Thus it would interest only those who were my comrades and my friends. Except for these, no one would read it to the end.

So much the better, for to think it would please those people whose conduct I blame would be enough to turn me away from writing. It would be painful for me that the humorous, sad or tragic images of our life should serve for the amusement of the indifferent or as an emotional outlet for shirkers.

I would not want such readers. They are not my kind. I attach no value to their astonishment, interest or admiration. I want to be understood by fighters and their esteem is more important for me than the finest crosses I could win.

And then, at bottom, you see, it is only pilots who can understand pilots. Civilians and soldiers understand nothing of it; never will they know what we think and what we are worth.

We do not have the same way of life, of talking, of fighting as the rest of the army.

The single fact that we like to dress elegantly and fancifully has lowered us in opinion twenty times more than if we had flinched on the day of an attack. Consider—to dress oneself neatly, work finished, when on the boulevards are seen drivers with helmet and gas mask and headquarters officers wearing trench boots freshly coated with mud to go on leave.

And then, we fly only three or four hours a day and, this done, we are at rest and out of danger. We are daily reproached for this complete relaxation after nerve-wracking strain by people who would be incapable of facing the fire of a machine gun or simply the daily risks of flying. That we do not sleep on bare ground troubles the nights of the old adjutants and the most insignificant road mender. Look, you speak of a bar: is it fitting for military men in the midst of war, at the front, to have a bar?

I don't know if we are military men, but certainly we are soldiers, if one accepts as the definition of a soldier a man who loves to fight, knows how to fight and knows how to die.

This tent-bar contributes to maintain the morale

at la Monnette. In the evenings after tough encounters, each regains his calm and gaiety, for the war stops for an instant; tomorrow it will start again and he will return with light heart to work and to danger.

Nervous pilots are not the ones to fight well and to knock down the Boche. Here, nerves are relaxed. We drink moderately, we play, we talk, and Decamps, the barman, keeps up camaraderie, gaiety and liveliness. I will always have in my ears the sound of his piano, a bit off key, which lulls our fatigue and makes us forget the uncertainties of tomorrow.

One evening (the very night before little Piétry was killed) a real musician came and played Grieg, Brahms, and Chopin for us—till midnight. No music has so moved me. But that is another story. The only story that is important to tell is that of the group. But to write it, one must have time. In order to have time, one must not fly and when one does not fly one no longer has any more right to speak of aviation than the mechanics of Bourget or of Plessis-Belleville.

"I have never been so afraid," said Cavel. "While I was diving on the first Boche, the second took me from the side and one of his bullets shattered my windshield. I got the pieces in my face. Without my goggles, I would have been blinded. Blood ran into my mouth, I didn't know what had happened to me . . ."

"As for me," said Dumarcet, "I was most frightened when I was on fire in the air in a chicken coop.* A back fire had ignited my carburetor. I dived like mad from 5500 to the ground looking

*The Farman plane; see note, p. 62. The motor was behind the pilot.

behind me at the flame which burned my rudder. Well, you know, when I landed . . ."

"As for me, it was when I got away on foot from the Boches. At the last village, nine kilometers from the frontier, the dogs barked and children started to run after me. They were trained for that because of the reward. I imagined myself recaptured after my sixteen days of tramping. I was afraid, afraid, I could not even walk anymore."

"Well, as for me," said Piston, "my greatest fright wasn't when I almost landed near Guiscard with a broken rod which had sheared my pan, nor when Lavisse was shot down in flames at my side. It was a day when that imbecile of a Guingasson took me for a spin in his cage and stunted like a louse to rattle me. Banked at ground level and amused himself with touching the tops of the poplars."

"That I was afraid is to say nothing. I was never so scared."

"Maybe it was because you never got used to vertical banks . . ."

 . . . April. Nothing can be compared with an airplane. Neither a bird in smooth flight, nor a buzzing insect resembles this clean human work, rectilinear, taut, which carries us.

The movements of the airplane, movements which have more strength and speed than ease, are not comparable to anything except perhaps at times to the precise trajectory of a light arrow pulled by a heavy tip.

No one knows what it is to fly, who, alone in the narrow seat of a single-seater, has not known the anxiety of the first acrobatics, the plane which climbs, which turns over, which is immobile for an instant before going into a whistling fall, the straining safety belt, the second during which he sees the ground behind his head, while he finds himself suspended at more than 12,000 feet in absolute emptiness and dizziness.

Now, every fighter pilot should be able to turn in all directions in the air, to spin, to loop, to pull straight up, to dive straight down. He should know how to turn upside down in combat without losing sight of the enemy, remain cool, and not lose his sense of direction when the ground seems to turn around him.

Our pursuit planes are well enough made so that all of these movements are possible for them. They are solid and balanced in such a fashion that, coming out of no matter what position, they will be diving, the motor in front.

Certainly, once the first apprehension is overcome, every pilot is capable of doing acrobatics; no one leaves Pau,* moreover, who has not done a wing over and a tail spin; but very few know how to do these stunts without damaging their planes, and it is the privilege of only a few aces to acquire precision in these manuevers and to find themselves, for example, lined up for firing behind a Boche after a wing over or a roll.

A fighter pilot who wants to improve himself must do acrobatics. It is necessary to become a kind of virtuoso if one wants to knock down the Boche. The physical anxiety which tightens the chest in the course of the first stunts must be overcome, and you must acquire cool-headedness, which only comes with long practice.

*Pau, where was located the school for final training of pilots, and which pursuit pilots were required to attend. J. B. V.

A plane returns. The motor hums, suddenly its song mounts in a crescendo, then abruptly stops, followed by a crackle of misfires.

Everyone looks up to see the exhibition. Up there the Spad turns about, jumps, does a wing over smoothly if the pilot is expert, heavily if he is awkward. What is he doing in his narrow cockpit, strapped in his seat?

Full throttle in pushing a bit to gather speed, then suddenly a thrust on the stick. The Spad climbs straight up, it bucks, tips over, is immobile for an instant. The pilot is on his back, he sees the ground behind his head, for an instant his throat tightens. Suddenly he cuts the gas, and gives a hard push with his foot.

On its back the plane goes head over tail, falls back on its nose by the weight of the motor, descends vertically, throws its passenger forward, almost out of his seat. He has only to pull back on the stick and hit the throttle.

Another wing roll. When the Spad is on its back, instead of letting the stick and rudder bar straighten up he keeps them deflected. The plane does not fall normally, but turns like a propellor around its axis. The earth seems to gyrate around the pilot, very rapidly. The tail spin.

Right in the middle, he comes out of the tail spin. One more roll. The plane is at 1500 feet. The motor cut, it approaches the ground. The Spad should land at normal speed, 100 or 120 kilometers per hour. It skims the ground swiftly at a foot or eighteen inches without yet touching, heading into the wind to brake more rapidly; it slows, it slows; the pilot holds it up in order to roll on the ground at the last moment; the wheels and the tail touch at almost the same time, the tail skid scrapes the strip, stops the plane, which, in a few feet, comes to rest. The Spad has landed and then rolls heavily toward the hangars.*

. . . April. Once again I come home with my machine gun jammed. In the middle of a fight with two single-seaters it stopped abruptly and I had to get clear of the two Fritz, Lord knows how.

Jamming! This is one of the major preoccupations of the pursuit pilot. Machine guns are delicate instruments, submitted to the violent shock of firing, vibrations of the motor, to the temperature and density of the atmosphere. Those on the Spads, moreover, fire between the blades of the propeller, thanks to a very delicate mechanism; thus there is not a more capricious arm; it stops working for a yes or a no, is always in danger of a breakdown no matter what care you take of it, and will desert you traitorously the moment you have most need of it.

A machine gun always fires on the ground; it rattles out its band of 200 cartridges without a hitch and Octave, bringing back my crate, says:

"You'll not tell me it's jammed this time, Lieutenant; it works like a charm."

Reassured, you take off. At 12,000 you stalk a pretty Boche who has come to take his little photos quietly and does not see you. The observer is leaning over the side and is not aware that a Spad is falling on him from above like a stone.

After diving 3000 feet, you are behind the

*In the original typescript this description was in the first person.

Boche. You aim; this one's in the bag. A palm,*
forty-eight hours leave, the girl friend . . ."

Clac, Clac.

Agitation in the enemy crate; the pilot pulls his
head between his shoulders and dives like mad,
straight down. The observer drops his camera,
which falls on his feet, fights with his turret,
which does not want to turn, taps the shoulder of
the pilot for him to dive less steeply, almost falls
overboard when the other corrects, loses his glove
and his goggles.

You say to yourself, "I really have that one."

But there is some doubt about that; at the third
shot your machine gun stops, the lever arm in the
air, while the Boche looms larger. You have to
avoid him and he is lost for this time.

Far from him, you shake your lever and breech,
but nothing works. Two cartridges are stuck,
rupture of a cartridge case or some piece broken,
and while you are looking for the breakdown, the
Boche has recovered his nerve and aims at you,
attacks furiously, and all you can do is flee, still
happy that some lurking single-seater does not
come and try to cut off your retreat.

There is no more painful impression, more ir-
ritating and more demoralizing than that of being
so brusquely deprived of your only means of attack and of defense and being nothing more than
an inoffensive crate at the mercy of the least
aggressive of the Boches.

And jamming is a daily accident; it ruins the
best chances and puts us in the worst messes. We
are happy when we find a good machine gun

*A palm frond is an added decoration on the ribbon of the
Croix de Guerre.

which we will never give up, and mechanics who know their business, who succeed in adjusting it. But no one can say that he is completely protected from a difficulty of this kind.

Yet one at last begins to know his weapon and its caprices and how to unjam it in flight; the stick between his knees, the louvre in the windshield open, one works at repairing the breakdown. Some aces have even dismounted their breech in full flight.

The major, who after all knows what a machine gun is and has not chosen the worst of the mechanics of the group, was caught short the other day under the stabilizer of a two-seater which he thought was a kill; I saw the fight, and the Boche, while fleeing towards his lines, fired on the big boss, who has not yet got over his anger; his encounter at least proves that he flies, attacks the Boches and does not run his group with his rear end on a chair shuffling unimportant papers.

# VII

. . . April. The big push is announced for these days. We know the big effort of the offensive is toward Fismes, where men and artillery are being accumulated and where the flight groups B . . ,* D. and M are assembled; meantime a serious push is also being prepared in Champagne.

Heavy shelling. Much artillery range spotting

*The group commanded by Major Brocard. J. B. V.

over the lines. But those among us who have seen Verdun and the Somme do not find that the pounding is the same as that which levels a terrain and renders it completely uninhabitable.

"Shell holes don't touch together," Bertrand says over and over.

. . . April. We are talking with Flippe, a comrade from the 721st, of the artillery preparation which is taking place.

"It is really too bad that my old observer Castillon is not here to give you some leads. There is not a better eye than his. I know what I'm talking about, having flown him over Verdun for eight months in my Mefeu."

"What's this about Castillon? I knew that fellow. Isn't he the observation officer of the la Pompelle section?"

"Observation officer of a sector, very likely; one never knows with a person like that who never writes. I've learned vaguely that he got his brevet at Plessis, but since then nothing. How do you know him?"

"That is not a story to repeat. One of our pilots the other day came across the first AR* of the army. He had never met such a crate, took him for a Boche, and jumped on top of him. Before he saw his cocards, he had already sent him a good burst which made some holes in his canvas near the passenger.

"You see the story. We rushed to make our excuses to the commandant of sector la Pompelle.

*AR, a new type of aircraft.

He took it all very well, no one was killed; the pilots and the observer shook hands and everything went off smoothly. That's how I made acquaintance with Observation Officer Castillon, who seemed to me very agreeable."

This evening, I am at la Pompelle sector, greeting Max as he gets out of his plane. He pilots a single-seater like a veteran, and has had a transmitter put on his Nieuport to do liaison and artillery spotting.

He has just returned from working with the artillery; at 1500 feet he saw trenches almost intact and people still in them. He is nervous.

An officer is there, doubtless responsible, for Max starts to call him to account.

"Captain, the preparation is incomplete, at least on the left of the sector; the third line and especially the V-shaped trenches are not demolished . . ."

But Max runs up against a smile of pity and a wall of incomprehension.

There are times, however, when a good observer in a plane, who has seen with his eyes the whole of the terrain can, alone of the whole army, have a precise idea of the work of the artillery in a sector. But this observer lacks the stripes to give him weight in a discussion.

"So it is you, Max, who is playing around in a Nieuport, in the evening, near Moronvilliers?"

"Yes, I was there yesterday."

"Did you see the two Albatroses which were lying in wait 900 feet above you?"

"What Albatroses?"

"And the Spad patrol which faced up to the Boches to see you were not slaughtered?"

"What Spads?"

The poor devil! He saw nothing. One fine day

when he is thinking of other things and looking somewhere else a Fritz will get behind him—clac, clac—shot down. He will not even know what happened.

I catch him and shake him. In a single-seater you have to look around you, look and look again. It is the only hope you have of getting out of it. You have to learn to see everything, to turn and twist your neck; life hangs on ten seconds of inattention.

But Max is not listening to me; he is giving his full attention to the artillery, and I understand his concern.


. . . April. The day of the attack.

It breaks in a thin fog which drifts under a low ceiling.

At 900 feet one is in the haze, at 1500 in the clouds. Nothing is more painful than to fly blindly in this way, with a milky curtain closed in front of you. Why is it that a romantic memory makes me think of the last battle of King Arthur?

Nothing to do, or almost. At the hour determined for the mission, I leave with Bertrand and de Loris, but the visibility is so bad that I lose them in a cloud and I find myself alone over the lines.

A seaplane crosses me, and I thought I was going to ram him, so suddenly did he come out of the mist, to disappear no less rapidly. For two hours I fly over the sector. At times I do not know where I am. From time to time planes from the Army Corps, Farmans, drop rockets over the confused terrain, destroyed woods and shell holes; or one of our patrols crosses me.

Suddenly I find myself nose to nose with a

Boche. He is as lost as I am; before I can line him up, he slips into a cloud and disappears.

De Loris, and the chief, who had separated, also have met several errant Fritz. Bertrand even thinks he knocked one down, but he was alone and no one will give him official confirmation of his victory.

Pasquin, the second lieutenant on whom the 757th placed many hopes and who, as officer cadet of the dragoons, had won the medaille militaire, has gone to knock down a balloon and has not returned.

Killed? Prisoner?


. . . April. At Moronvilliers, at Mont-Haut, at Cornillet, at Casque, our lines have advanced a good four or five kilometers. The battle continues.

The group has made a collective show; two escadrilles have climbed to the west and have come up to the lines at 12,000 feet near Reims; two others including the 705th, left by way of the Argonne, have made a large circuit to the north, reached Machault and rejoined the first near Pont-Faverger.

Naturally, there was no question of Boches; the rare ones we saw fled without wanting to tangle with so dense a formation.

But this evening they answered us in kind; the three patrols of the escadrille were staggered at 7500, 10,500, and 13,500 when twelve single-seaters jumped us.

It was a great melee. The Albatroses attacked the intermediary patrol of three Spads where I found myself; each of us was tackled by two or three adversaries and we got out of the affair as best we could.

I saw Chelcher do a roll, then a tail spin, and I thought he was shot down. Legrand imitated him; as for myself, two Albatroses dived on me from above and their four machine guns made an unmusical sound in my ears. I disentangled myself from my Fritz by flat turns, without banking and by a few spins.

No matter what, we were properly shaken up and we found ourselves at 6000, almost at the Roman road with a band of Fritz over our heads who quietly sauntered four kilometers in our lines, while the upper patrol, composed of only two Spads, circled at 13,500 not daring to attack this gang alone.

I was furious. Bertrand, who showed up alone over the lines to see the work of his escadrille, arrived just in the nick of time. He helped me round up everybody, and it wasn't especially easy, for in the air there is no command possible by voice or gesture; finally, however, seven Spads found themselves in a single group which gained altitude to go nip the Boches.

We went against the Albatroses, then a bit dispersed, and each of us started to fire on the one he chose. They did not resist, although they were more numerous and had the altitude; they returned home without accepting combat. But Legrand hit one, who went into a spin to the ground, where he burned. There was another which we thought we had shot down; he was diving on me when Bertrand got under his tail and hit him from very close range. The Boche went straight down from 10,500 to 3000. There, he straightened out and flew over the lines like a shot.

At this time, the group, alerted by the balloons, sent us reinforcements. They flew toward the enemy squadron which had reformed over its lines and the battle started again. I think that P . . shot down another Albatros; in any case the Boches were swept away in a jiffy.

As for ourselves, we were exhausted by these combats, these changes of altitude and by two hours of flight; in addition, we were nearly out of gas.

We returned to the field.

# VIII

. . . April. Coco has not returned.

For two months he was the combat comrade of Piston. They always flew together with the sole preoccupation, the fixed idea of knocking down a Boche. But they had the fault of flying to hell and gone over enemy territory.

"You are going to get cornered," Bertrand often said, "your motor will conk out, or three or four single-seaters will surprise you, do a scalp dance around you, and will not let you go."

But they wanted to have their Boche and looked for him too far away.

At noon, they left. A few instants after taking off, Piston had some motor trouble and had to land. Coco went on alone. He was not seen again.

How did he fall? Perhaps, inattentive for an instant, he heard bullets clattering around him. He had no time to understand, to resist. He was already wounded, his plane in flames already was tumbling down.

Perhaps also, the Boches surrounded him in numbers and cut off his retreat. He fought, but in the unequal battle two enemies fired from behind when he tried to line up a third one. He was harassed from all sides. Before falling, did he have time to feel his abandonment, the anguish, the despair, all the cruelty of this inescapable fate?

. . . April. Here it is more than a year that I have been fighting in the air, and I have still not been able to get a clear idea of the worth and the mentality of my enemies, the German aviators.

They seem to me extraordinarily unequal and I have not found among them the homogeneity which characterizes us. With them we go from the very good to the very bad without transition. At times one meets a crew or a single-seater which will fight like a lion and commands admiration, at other times the worst sort of people who lose their nerve, abandon their mission or desert the crate they are accompanying, at the first sign of danger.

First of all one must correct this ridiculous assertion according to which German pilots are cowardly because in combat they seek to be several against one and to gain victory without risk in ganging up on an isolated and panic-stricken individual.

That is good practice in war; and the war we have to fight is not sentimental. It is our strict duty to hunt and destroy the most enemies possible with the minimum of losses, and we should employ a bit more of the Boelke and Richthoffen system.

Moreover, when three Frenchmen corner a Boche ten kilometers from his lines, they do all they can to knock him down and don't stop at the thought that this unequal duel is neither elegant nor chivalrous.

But aside from this question, do German aviators have more nerve than ours?

There are some admirable ones, who fight with magnificent courage and knock down numerous of our planes. But, as a general rule, when the numbers are equal, the Boche always gives way to the French, at least to French pursuit planes. Here, in Champagne, eight enemy planes regularly turn tail before four or five Spads. It is usual for two of us to fly over the lines or even within the German lines while above there is a patrol of four single-seaters which do not attack us.

The Germans make only short sorties against us and do most of their work within their lines. On the contrary, a French pursuit plane never takes off without making a turn over German territory. Unless the numerical inferiority is very great, all of our patrols go into enemy territory two, four, or six kilometers from our trenches. Here, we constantly fly above Nauroy and even Pont-Faverger.

Nevertheless there must be a very strict and hard discipline in German aviation. This comes out in talking with prisoners, some of whom have gone out under orders, alone, on long distance missions from which they were sure not to return.

But where the Boches especially show less nerve than we, are less "aviators," is in not taking advantage of the superiority of their equipment; for though our pursuit planes are largely equal to theirs, they should make a hecatomb of our Army Corps planes, Farmans and Caudrons, much inferior to theirs which do the same work.

We have all dreamed of meeting German Farmans. We would have shot them down like sitting ducks. Courage and unshakable morale were needed and are still needed for our pilots of the Army Corps to hold out on those barges.

There was a time, in 1915, when we had the G.3, the Henry Farman and the 70 hp cages, while the Aviatiks, the L.V.G. and the Albatros were about equal to 23 meter Nieuports which we were still using for pursuit at the start of the attacks on Verdun.

If the roles had been reversed, our pilots and observers would have hit the German aviation so hard that it would never have recovered from our blows.

I do not undervalue my enemy, that would be to depreciate myself, but I am absolutely sure that the Boches are not equal to us and that they are infinitely less aviators, less pilots, less pursuit fliers, than we are, who are fliers to our fingertips.

"Don't go there, it won't do any good to see that, he's pulp."

"Who is it?"

"A non-commissioned officer of ours. He had been here for ten days. He wanted to bank on take off, his plane went over on its wing and hit the ground."

And Dumarcet adds:

"That's the fifth in two weeks. The four others took off on patrol. Pfutt! not a one left, vaporized, disappeared, we never saw them again.

"Those who were in the air with them said: 'Hasn't so and so landed? What happened to him? He was on my right at the start of the barrage, suddenly I no longer saw him. I thought that he had motor trouble. What happened to him? And we didn't even have a fight!'

"And that is all that is known of them. No, come to think about it, we heard from one of them; he landed at an aerodrome, near Juniville, among the Fritz, thinking he was here on our field. And he had the gall to drop me a word with my name, my grade, my squadron, the sector and everything, to tell me that he was not injured and that he simply had made a mistake. Can you imagine that?

"For the others, nothing. The balloons speak vaguely of seeing smoke trails far over the lines. They must have separated from the patrol, tried to do some hunting on their own, to get a Boche for themselves, and it was the Boche who got them.

"You see, among us, there are too many losses among the young. If I ever command an escadrille —and why not?—there are two things on which I have determined and on which I will be inflexible:

"None of my people will stunt at ground level.

"Never will a pilot stay alone over the lines.

"No matter the quality of my good fellows, the rule will be absolute. Because we have too often tolerated this double imprudence we have seen the best ones get themselves killed or get shot down uselessly.

"The old pilots are too sure of themselves. They think they can get away with anything, and vanity helping, stunt at ground level. Invariably they get what's coming to them; a bank on take off, a slip over at too low altitude; coming out of a spin too late, goodbye! We pick them up with a spoon.

"All the more reason that the young should not indulge in any foolishness, not the least stunting at less than 1000 feet (above that everything can and should be allowed with a Nieuport and a Spad), but it is the devil and all to prevent them from doing foolish things to impress the gallery.

"The same for group flights. The single-seaters have every advantage in flying as a group. They thus increase their means of attack and of defense and diminish the chances of surprise. You know it doesn't take very long to get a crate on your neck without having had the time to see it—"

"Yes, two planes flying at 150 kilometers per hour come toward each other at 300. But a crate which is coming toward you head on is scarcely visible at more than two kilometers and a half or three kilometers. At 300 an hour, a kilometer takes twelve seconds; thus a Boche, from the moment he becomes visible, is on you in a period which varies between 24 and 36 seconds."

"That's about it. Thus, no room for mistakes; it is better to be two or three to watch than only one. A single-seater never should go alone over the lines; it is playing the game of the Boche and is putting itself at his mercy. But no one wants to understand that; the veterans want to hunt individually, through overconfidence and a desire to work on their own; the novices imitate them through vanity and ignorance."

"And both finish up by being killed, the young by a lack of address and training, the veterans because the pitcher that often goes to the well gets broken at last."

"The pitcher! you said the word, the pitcher!* [It's us who are pitchers, old man, pitchers to make war from the first day, to return wounded, worn, while numberless around us save their skins in soft berths.]

"Pitchers also to love this dirty job as we love it, this job which, through crack up, bullet or shell, will certainly knock us off, inevitably, one fine evening or one fine morning. . . . . . . . . . . . . . . . . . . . .
. . . . . . . . . . . . . . . . . . . . . . . . . . . . . . . . . . . . . . . . ."

"Yes, but I am still hanging on and I want to hang on, and you hang on, and others, more numerous than you think, have been hanging on since the first day.

"Moreover, who would hang on if we did not? In aviation, we are all bourgeois; those who were not have become so and will remain so. To whom can we say hang on, if the bourgeois do not? We are bourgeois and our arm is a privileged one, a bourgeois among the other arms. Pay, lodging, clean hands, interesting work, chivalric single combat, rewards, hopes of citation in dispatches,** all those privileges.

"But be very careful not to take these privileges from us, not to reduce aviation to poverty, to strict discipline, to drab common obscurity; you will risk taking from it its strength and its secret energies.

"You know very well, we are considered ama-

---

*A play on words: "pitcher" (cruche) also means "fool."

**Lt. Villars received five citations in the War of 1914-1918. He was also once cited in the Second World War.

teurs; our independence is reproached, our youth, our uniforms, our easy manners, the camaraderie which reigns among us between the ranks; we are especially reproached for not being military.

"Some go into a faint when they see a flier's jacket. Others become indignant when they visit an airfield, at the good fellowship, the freedom which prevails, especially at those little groups of planes that take off without possible supervision and that for two hours are answerable only to their sense of duty.

"Do they believe, when they have militarized our arm, that all will be for the better? When they will have put infantry adjutants, made captains after years of service, and old scrubbed-up cavalry majors in our units; when the crates will do column right, when the pilots will line up for review and will be dressed by the quartermaster, when the mechanics will spring to attention, a wrench in one hand and an oil can in the other, do they think that aviation will have gained very much?

"Still it must be understood that we are not a crowd, but a gathering of individuals. That's a difference not to be sneezed at.

"The strength and buoyancy of our branch is in our freedom and our imagination, in our young chiefs, in our pilots, even younger, loving to fight as they love to enjoy themselves. We are the refuge of all those who fear a too narrow spirit, the discipline of a regular corps, who dread waiting and boredom and who still want to serve, who love danger and adventure. Those, the individualists, come to us. What matters their open collar, their love of Paris, their ignorance of certain military usages! These are eccentricities, not serious vices. On the ground, they wear pull-overs, big shoes and, once in their single-seater, a stick in their hand, a machine gun in front of them, they are real soldiers.

"It should not be forgotten that these gay little dogs fight alone, at 12,000 feet, in a crate of wood and canvas, shot at with incendiary bullets. You will find their numberless graves from Dunkirk to Belfort, which shows they well know how to serve.

"If you bother them too much, if you make playthings of them in the hands of a brigadier de semaine,* many of them will leave who have no military obligation, being unfit, discharged, or of the auxiliaries; as for those who will remain, they will become no better, rather the contrary.

"Look at the major; he has understood that very well. For what does not concern courage and discipline under fire, he has the greatest indulgence, and pilots who are not plagued by petty nagging are well mannered and amenable to discipline. None of the group would knock down cops in the streets of Paris,** but no one either who would not find it natural simply to ask a favor or advice from the big chief.

"The major well knows that not just anybody can be a real pursuit pilot. He does not have too many good fliers; those he has, he hangs onto. The most eccentric are often the best; we need individualities who are energetic and seasoned.

"The chief is not concerned with our arm of

---

*A non-commissioned officer of the week.
**Reference to an incident which had caused a scandal. A pilot, Navarre, fought with police in a music hall. Navarre, whom I knew, was a remarkable flier, but half mad. J. B. V.

[214]

origin, the paper we read, nor the length of our hair; perhaps he does not know if you are from the regular army or the reserve; all he asks is that we be brave and willing; he knows if our patrols leave on time and if we attack the Boche; he knows what we have in us.

"And so, look at the results, the work done by the group, its homogeneity, its fire, its morale. Especially its morale! Can you imagine a better morale in a unit which has suffered such heavy losses, almost all in dead and disappeared, and which nevertheless keeps so much drive that it is necessary to slow down certain pilots who want to fly additional patrol hours or who attack the Boche too imprudently.

"It is very fortunate the pilots of single-seaters are so eager, for if they did not feel so how could they be made to face such danger!

"Happily, there are among us factors which maintain morale and gaiety no matter what the sacrifices are.

"In aviation, already privileged, we are the privileged.

"Privileged in recruitment. We are sent the youngest, the most spirited, the most skilled pilots, top drawer of the schools.

"Privileged for equipment. We have the best planes, the soundest, the fastest, the best balanced, the most agreeable to fly. In these crates we can allow ourselves anything. We really feel we have a capacity unknown to the rest of humanity—flying."

"Without mentioning the official citation, of which everyone is so desirous."

"The citation if you like, but it is reserved for a few exceptional characters. It's far beyond us; I admit that I don't think much about it. I will easily console myself for not having been a brilliant pilot, if I can say to myself that I was a pilot who did his duty.

"That which especially keeps the morale of the single-seater pilot high when so many around him are being shot down is that he relies on his experience, his coolness, his professional skill to get out of a scrape.

"While in other branches personal valor can hardly shield one from blows, with us it has a primary importance in evading wounds and death.

"Nieuport and Spad, being solid and well balanced, will do us in by accident only if we commit an imprudence, error or a fault.

"In combat, our dexterity also preserves us, for we have the initiative of the attack, we choose the instant and the place, we have the speed and the mobility which allow us to maneuver around the enemy and to evade his blows, and each one thus hopes to be saved by his skill and cleverness.

"That is why, losing more than the rest of aviation, we maintain our morale. That is why we have such a love for our profession.

"For we love it, this profession. We are perhaps the only arm which, after three years of war, still enthusiastically does what we have to do. There are pilots who would sing the joy of flying and the joy of fighting if lyricism and poetic language were not so far from our character and our outlook.

"But you know how one becomes prosaic in taking care of magnetos, oil pumps, and carburetor jets. We scarcely express our feelings. Our strongest emotions, excitements, admiration,

Victory Confirmed

patriotism, the deep anguish, the finest spectacles, admiration and pity for the infantrymen, the buddies who fall, the perpetual danger—we never speak of all that, through dislike of being bombastic. Our fear of big words makes us cover our feelings with indifference, coldness or irony.

"This is why we do not exalt our profession; it is not because we don't love it, for some among us love it like a vice. Like a vice we would be incapable of quitting, and still we are sure that one day or another, inevitably, it will do us in."

# IX

. . . April. Yesterday, it was Cavel who came home triumphant. Bertrand had allowed him to go out with Piston between barrages. A single-seater had attacked the latter and Cavel found himself just behind the Fritz, who was diving. He fired—a few rounds of machine gun fire—and the Boche, breaking up in the sky, flew to pieces.

Today, it is Chelcher. He landed, rolled to the hangars, with difficulty got his spindly legs out of his seat and cried to me:

"I got one!"

"A Fritz?"

"Two-seater in a spin over Nauroy. Look, he left some bullets in my wing. The machine gunner was still firing when he started to fall."

"So that's how you go amuse yourself, leaving me to worry at the Bessonneaus. Come and tell your little story at the intelligence tent."

(My motor refused to start on time and I couldn't fly this morning.)

The major joyfully welcomes us; he rubs his hands, walks into the tent, congratulates Chelcher, orders that his taxi be prepared, goes outside and takes a few steps with us.

"I know very well that it is hard; we have losses in the group; every day comrades are shot down, but we are also doing work, good work. The Boche strikes, but we strike harder than he. For one pilot of the G.C.* shot down, there are three Fritz done in in flames or in pieces or knocked down behind our lines. P . . . knocks them down in series, one a day. And we do not exaggerate confirmations here; I'm close-fisted when it comes to crediting Boches to the pilots, but at least a plane which we say has been shot down is really finished. During this time, the planes of the C.A. are so undisturbed they frisk over the lines; the Farman's are no longer shot down, and if anyone gets it, we do. So much the better, my friends, for we are made for that!"

> "You will fear neither the incendiary bullet nor the Boche who comes stealthily, nor the demon noon-day sun."

. . . April. "Hey!"

"What's that? Ah! It's you, Lieutenant."

"It's a quarter to twelve. Patrol!"

"We're ready."

The occupants of the tent get up, stretch, with bowed backs, stiff legs, hollow faces.

"What heat for April!"

*Groupe de Chasse (Pursuit Group).

For a week the weather has been like that of mid-summer, stifling; we are overcome with fatigue and the heat; we sleep constantly and we no longer eat anything except eggs and pickles washed down by the rosé of the district. Our appearance reflects this.

The clay soil of Champagne, baked by the sun, crumbles under foot like cinders. The wind sock on the Bessonneau hangs limp; heat waves dance over the ground. Noon.

The smell of hot oil around the planes upsets one's stomach.

The canvas flying suit, silk stocking, helmet, goggles. Pull out the chocks!

But my Spad had idled too long, the thermometer is at seventy degrees; when I will have taxied to take off it will be at eighty degrees; I will not be able to climb without burning out my motor.

But one has to leave, for it is time. I take off. A heat pocket almost pancakes me on the pine wood, at the end of the field. I climb, with excess speed, concerned about my motor whose water is on the verge of boiling, not daring to pull back on the stick.

Finally 4500 feet! The thermometer stops rising, its needle steadies, the patrol gathers around me, we reach the front.

Sun and solitude. A blue sky, almost somber, weighs upon us. One hand to shield our eyes, we hunt the Boche invisible in the light. Our dazzled eyes see green and gold disks on everything.

Under the torpor of noon the lines sleep: infantrymen, artillerymen, even aviators, for not a single crate appears; that balloon which slowly turns on its cable must have been forgotten. We

fly aimlessly, the only living and moving beings
in this motionless landscape.

The German pilots at Juniville or Machault,
stretched out in their rocking chairs, smoke their
cigars and drink their coffee. I have been told that
this coffee is made of acorns and the cigars of
walnut leaves; but there is still the rocking chair
which I envy them, for my back is wedged in a
hard and narrow seat which a cushion does not
soften, a sentimental souvenir, but too light as
padding.

We are alone . . .

No.—Boom!

At three thousand feet from us a shrapnel explodes, blooms, all white. We look at it almost
tenderly; it alone pays attention to us.

Overcome with this effort, the mobile cannon
fall silent, exhausted.

A Boche, a little Boche, only send us a little
Boche, that this dismal countryside may return to
life and action, that we may shake off the weight
of this solitude, of this light, especially of this
light!

*A sagitta volante in die, a negotio perambulante in tene-
bris, ab incursu et daemonio meridiano.**

A novelist has used this rich phrase, taken its
force and its beauty from it. "Demon of noon"**
he has said, "image of temptations which assail
a mature man and disturb his senses."

It was unnecessary to look so far for so common a translation. The demon of noon, is not
allegorical; ask those who have felt on their

*The arrow that flieth by day, etc., the familiar line from
the 91st Psalm.
**Title of a mediocre novel by Paul Bourget. J. B. V.

[222]

shoulders its force and its weight. Those also know the flying bullet, the danger which comes so quietly—the demon of noon!

Minutes, quarter hours, hours . . .

Cavel, on my right, suddenly climbs vertically; his plane flips over, is motionless for an instant at my altitude, wheels in the air, then suddenly dives toward the ground in a side-slip.

"When the patrol is finished, I will let you know by a wing-over," he told me. Indeed, it is time. From the direction of Souain three dark dots approach which come to relieve us. It seems that with them the world awakens and lives anew.

A turn to the right toward the field—slackening of taut nerves—relief, the end.

The return . . .


. . . April. "We went to visit the Boche of Sagny. The poor fellow is in terrible shape. One should not go to see things like that."

"Sagny shot down a Boche?"

"You weren't flying during the patrol a while ago?"

"Me? Yes. I got myself shot up by a big two-seater who, incidentally, got it too, seriously enough. I even thought I had knocked him down, but it seems not; the balloons did not indicate anything."

"As for Sagny, there is no mistake; the patrol cornered a little single-seater over d'Auberive. Loris attacked it first, and missed; then Sagny dived and must have made a hit, for a great deal of black smoke came out of its motor. The pilot started to spin down as fast as he could to try to land before being seared by the flames, but all of a sudden the plane started to tail spin and crashed on the Roman road. Everything burned on the ground."

"It's odd, isn't it, this vitality of airplanes. In order to knock them down, it is necessary to hit certain points exactly—the head, the chest of the pilot, or the gas tank. If not, the machine continues on its way, indifferent and insensible. But if you hit a vulnerable organ, pfutt! the plane no longer lives, nothing directs it any longer. Everything collapses and goes to pieces. The life of a pilot is worth but little."

"Yes, we have been to see the German and his crate, but he fell within sight of the lines; when we had assembled around the debris, the German artillery started to fire and we had to leave."

"Too bad, you could have taken away the machine gun."


. . . 30 April. I had not seen that particular Boche coming; he came in front of me and I took him for a Sop, but suddenly Bertrand, with whom I was patrolling, dived in his direction and attacked him.

As usual, Bertrand was going full tilt. He fired while boring in full speed on the Fritz. He was closer and closer to him, close enough to touch him, too close . . .

I did not quite grasp what happened: The Boche made a sudden turn, something broke in the Spad of my comrade, pieces of wood and of canvas fell all around and Bertrand began a flat vertical fall, certainly knocked down.

In a flash, it crossed my mind: "My chief is shot down." At once I understood that nothing was to be gained by diving behind him to pick him up.

I had only one idea—get the Boche in his turn.

The Boche dived full speed for his lines. I dived after him. Never did I descend so rapidly, like an arrow, like a falling stone. My head was wrenched backward and my body projected over the upper wing.

I caught up with the two-seater, I fired, keeping straight in line with him, but he immediately began to spiral; I could keep him in my line of sight only briefly. Still I did not let go of him.

I was very close, I circled around him without concern for his rear machine gun, but I did not hear it fire. It was incomprehensible. I looked closer and this is what I saw:

The machine gun turned in the wind without anyone holding it; the passenger, collapsed on the bottom of his seat, was dead, killed by the bullets of Bertrand, and his body was thrown about with the veering of the plane.

At this moment, the pilot leaned backwards, held out his arm and signaled for me not to fire any more; he was giving up. He turned toward the south to land in our lines.

It was a spectacle, "never seen," this big machine, the immense black crosses, disarmed, very close, vanquished; this dead man, and the panic-stricken pilot saying *Kamerad* "in the air."

I had attacked at over 12,000 feet; at 9000 Cavel joined me. He fired at first, then he understood what was happening and contented himself with circling the plane. From time to time, the pilot, with a burst of energy, made a movement toward his lines, but our bullets drove him to the south.

At 1500 feet, the Boche, Cavel, and I were near Prosnes. The appearance of the ground, which was coming up, brusquely brought me back to reality. I looked at my thermometer; it was at sixteen or eighteen, pressure was zero. I was about to hit the throttle, when there were a few sputterings, and suddenly I saw in front of me my propellor crossed, motionless.

I was literally snatched from the fight, for my Spad, motorless, began to drop rapidly, and without losing an instant, I had to find a place to land.

Cavel at the same time had the same misadventure; his motor had also given out, but without stopping altogether, and he followed me in having to abandon our adversary a few hundred feet from the ground.

The Boche found himself alone, free, without enemies, after this hard fight. I imagine that he must have looked around; he saw himself disengaged and put on the gas to regain his lines.

But he was doomed; his tank, riddled by bullets, had allowed gas to run over the motor; at the first firing of the engine the fumes ignited, the flames enveloped the machine, which fell over the trenches, grilled in the wink of an eye.

For myself, I did not see his end. Worried, I lost altitude, hunting for a spot to set down. My ears whistled after this wild descent, I had the impression that my head was going to burst; in any case, it seemed to me that my eyes, which I felt pushed out of my head, would never go back into their sockets.

A square clearing, freshly cut in a pine wood. I direct myself toward this refuge; there are several shell holes, I will dodge them. I am going to land my crate a little high; it skims over the ground, it skims, I arch my back, I wait. The earth goes by less rapidly, my Spad touches down, the tail skid first, then the wheels; it is still going quite fast scraping the bumps, and suddenly something throws me forward, I see the five fingers of my hand instinctively put in front of me to protect my face . . . then . . .

Here I am prone on a cot; a strange face, a bit anxious, leans over me, while a hand pours a stream of cold water in my ear.

"You flipped over in a shell hole. Do you feel better?"

"Ça va."

"Your belt broke, that's why you're bleeding; you fell face forward; you are gashed under your eye and on the right cheek."

"I well know it."

An artillery captain, excellent man, offers me his wash basin to check the blood which runs from my face, then he shares his breakfast with me. A few minutes later, I am on my feet.

I jump for the telephone: "Hello! and Lt. Bertrand?"

"He's OK. He flew into the tail skid of the Boche, a part of the wing was broken between the leading edge and the longeron, all of the upper canvas was pulled off; the Spad which no longer had enough surface to carry it, went straight down like an elevator. All during the fall the lieutenant was saying, 'This is it, this time I have it for good.'

"But he managed to set his machine down flat, breaking his two wheels and the tail skid, nothing more. He got out of it well shaken up. And you?"

"Me, I'm OK. Nothing serious, the taxi on its back, two wings and a propellor to change."

My rescuer, the artillery captain, takes me back

by car over dusty roads. Mourmelon, the camp of Chalons . . . the sun burns my face, my cheek laid open, my swollen eye; my wrist hurts.

Here is Bertrand, holding out his hands.

"My old chief!"

"Mon vieux!"

For if we are up to paying the bill when it is due, we still like to see it put off to a future date.

# X

"I have a friend, almost a brother, who serves in an alpine battalion. At the Somme, he got a shell splinter in the leg. He is at the rest camp. He said to his commander the other day: 'I want to make a request to transfer into aviation'; to which this senior officer answered: 'What the hell are you going to do there? You want to make war for the women and the journalists?' This story is for you, Flippe, handsome young buck looking for a citation."

"If I have fought only for women and journalists," answered Flippe, "I have been robbed, having chiefly, as concerns boudoirs, known Adrian huts where one is too hot or too cold, and up to now having missed the honor of public notice."

"Tell it, my friend, cry it from the roof tops, you will still not change ideas anchored in the head of the ordinary infantryman. For the man of the trenches, the aviator is an unknown and suspect animal. The poilu is ignorant of our role, our work, and our losses. Aviation is as far from him as Venezuelan diplomacy or the tax collecting system of Indo-China. Still, we are of some importance in battle. It is distressing that the infantry knows nothing about us. Among the thousand directives sent each morning to the company commanders, for pity's sake, let someone slip in a three-page summary which would give the infantrymen some idea of what a squadron, plane, observer, and pilot are."

And Martigues:

"Last week, I had two days to go see my brother in the Astoria hospital. He is a non-commissioned officer in the 703rd and got a bullet in his foot at Craonne.

"At Épernay a lieutenant colonel of the Zouaves got into my compartment. Young, tall, smartly dressed, a rosette, shoulder knot and the rest. He sat in front of me, saw my pilot's wings; he coughed, fidgeted and finally he could not contain himself and said:"

"You sure did a great job at Chemin des Dames, you fellows in the aviation! Every morning there were enemy planes spotting our positions. Because of that, on April 17 I lost half of my officers. Last month, I had the finest regiment in the world, now . . . you fellows take it easy up there. You don't know what it's like with the effectives who have to take a beating."

"I replied politely to him, to this man whose concern was deep and sincere:

"Mon colonel, you are wrong if you think that we are having fun on the days of attack in dodging among the shells. I know very well that you have terrible losses in the infantry, but we also have

[229]

lost a good number of fine men during these last months. When you return from leave, come make a tour of our squadrons; they will be much flattered. When you have been told what each of them has lost, I am sure that you will shake the hands of the survivors without thinking you are dishonoring yourself."

"Very well, but how do you explain that, if aviation is doing its job, the Boches come over our trenches without being shot down?"

"Mon colonel, it would take a while to explain; still, if it doesn't bore you . . ."

"Go right ahead."

"Here's how it is. In order to watch seriously the front of which you speak and to prevent the incursion of enemy planes, alone or in groups it would take a minimum of three patrols of six single-seaters each, staggered at different heights. That is, to have permanently twenty or so planes over the lines.

"Each plane has two hours of fuel in its tank; it can work twice a day; that is, four hours of flight.

"But climbing, going and returning to the field from the lines shortens the time of the sortie, and the planes remain effectively over the trenches only an hour and a half each time, or *three hours* in all for each.

"Now, at this time of the year, between 4:30 a.m. and 8:00 p.m. there are fifteen or sixteen hours of daylight. Thus more than five groups of twenty planes each are needed to maintain a watch over the front, or in round numbers, ten or so squadrons of a dozen single-seaters.

"On the other hand, you know that planes don't run like sewing machines. There are continual breakdowns; motors to dismount or to change, air frames to adjust or straighten up, without speaking of the daily losses in materiel and men. A normal squadron which flies every day can put only half of its effectives over the line. It is a loss which seems enormous to strangers, but those of the profession know this is not excessive and that many units will exceed this proportion.

"Thus it is not ten squadrons which we would need, but twenty or so to protect a front of fifty kilometers. Now, we are unfortunately very far from having such a great number of units in the sectors of attack. The Boches, incidentally, are in the same situation as we.

"But that is not all . . .

"Was he still listening, your Zouave?"

"Certainly, he was fascinated. He caught on very well, that lieutenant-colonel. He saw that I was not kidding him and he listened with wide open ears. I then told him:

"Even if we could accumulate twenty or so squadrons in the region of which we speak, do you think that we could assure absolute security? I maintain on the contrary that some Boches would inevitably escape from our observation, would slip between the meshes of the net, no matter what the quality and conscientiousness of the pilots in service.

"First, there are Boches who would get in from below. A German aviator will not hesitate to cruise two hours over his lines, waiting for the favorable moment when the sky will be free. This moment necessarily comes. When the lower patrol is at one end of its sector, it will take it four or five minutes to get back to the other (providing there is no head wind). Even going at 150 kilometers an hour, one does not cover twelve kilometers in ten seconds. Our low-flying enemy will thus have four or five minutes to make a swing of three kilometers over our lines, take his photo of the trenches, machine gun our infantrymen and drop back home at 600 feet protected by his anti-aircraft guns. After that, chase after him!

"There will also be the Boches who will get through from above. It's possible, once a week, to stay two hours at 18,000 feet, but it's impossible for a human to do two patrols daily of an hour and a half at that altitude. People like Guynemer or Dorme perhaps could hold out, but one cannot ask ordinary mortals to have the exceptional lungs and fierce wills of these demi-gods.

"Our Spads, moreover, have difficulty in climbing higher than 15,000 or 16,500. During our patrols we stay between 12,000 and 15,000, or else we will give out rapidly. The Boche two-seaters, which, specially constructed for this kind of reconnaissance, are less rapid, but have more wingspread than our single-seaters, choose their moment, take a long time to gain altitude and slide in front of our noses without it being possible, most of the time, to catch them.

"It is thus that a Fritz goes, once or twice a week, over Chalons. No one can reach him and the Chalonnais are persuaded that we let him by because we lack nerve.

"That's not all . . ."

"More!"

"Suppose, mon colonel, that your twenty squadrons, flying continually with 200 planes, denied isolated or small patrols access to the lines, would you be rid of Boche observers? Would your positions be sheltered from their nervy spotting?

"When you tie up more than 200 crates on a

narrow front, the Germans will have brought only thirty planes, three escadrilles. They will group them around two photo two-seaters and will fly at what altitude pleases them and make a sweep over your sector. This large formation will fall on your isolated patrols, will shake them up, and before home base, the pursuit group, sends reinforcements, the band of Fritz will have finished its work, will have flown over our lines during a quarter of an hour or twenty minutes, taken photos and gathered its information."

"But then, young man, you are condemning pursuit aviation; you say yourself that it cannot guarantee the performance of its mission."

"I beg your pardon, mon colonel, it can assure its mission, but this mission is not that which is generally thought.

"If you want to tie down groups to one task in one place continually, hold them to eternal patrols over the lines, you will immobilize a large number of effectives and you will be disappointed to boot, for trying to stop all of the enemy planes is trying to keep all the water in a sieve.

"If, on the contrary, you employ your combat aviation in a more tactical fashion, you will not be let down.

"Ask of them in normal times:

"To protect planes of the Army Corps and of the army, either when they work over the lines, or during long distance reconnaissance;

"To gain moral superiority over the enemy in harassing them constantly during their missions, in inflicting losses each time the occasion presents itself, in sending offensive patrols several kilometers over their lines.

"Ask of them on days of attack:

"To take off en-masse, to increase their activity, to take complete mastery of the air, to sweep momentarily all enemy machines from the zone of the offensive, an intense effort which they can sustain only a few hours and which will not be possible if you have not economized your effectives before the attack.

"To sum up, we are a bit in the situation of the artillery. The batteries pound the enemy gun positions, trying to render life untenable. On certain days, through an activity momentarily intensified, they almost completely silence the enemy, but in ordinary times the infantrymen do not blame the artillerymen when they receive a shell. They should not accuse the aviators when they see a Boche over their heads.

"We are used to the fact that we are much maligned. The poorest drivers and the most ignorant civilians make judgments on us, blame us, criticize our way of life, criticize our role in battle: 'The trouble with aviators is . . .' 'They would be perfect if . . .' 'It's outrageous to see that . . .' and such tripe. These vituperations, half stupidity and half jealousy, rest lightly on our shoulders. On the other hand, it is vexing to be criticized not by the shirkers or civilians, but by front-line troops who are generally full of distrust of air fighters.

"But alone we share with the infantrymen the perpetual risk which kills us daily, crushing losses, and finally the privilege of 'seeing the Boche,' knowing his true color, and delivering blows on him at first hand.

"That is why, mon colonel, it is necessary to admit that when things are not as they should be, it is not always our fault. If your Zouaves, the day of attack, suffer large losses, are stopped, do not reach their objective, no one says, 'They have not done their job'; don't think that we have done ours with bad grace. It is not always easy. We also have taken heavy blows—fatigue, comrades who fall, effectives which melt away. Give us then a bit of credit, pity us as you pity your people and have confidence in us.

"At this moment, the steward from the wagon-restaurant came to call us. The lieutenant-colonel took me to his table; he was all solicitude and all camaraderie. A great guy, I tell you. He called me his little friend and offered a fine cognac and a cigar, saying, 'Between soldiers.'

"Our intimacy reached its peak when I told him I was going to Paris to see my young pilot brother half done in at Craonne, and that I myself had a shell splinter in my lung when I was a second lieutenant of infantry, and a bullet in the neck as an observer in a two-seater. He whispered into my ear:"

"I have a nephew of seventeen and a half, a nice little fellow, who has the devil in his bones. He has only a single idea, to join up—in the aviation, naturally. My sister and I insist that he wait a little while yet. You understand, in that branch . . . his family . . ."

. . . May. "You are shaken up and a nervous wreck, you are no longer doing anything worthwhile and your face looks like a pudding. Leave, take twenty-four hours in Paris; that will put you back on your feet."

"And you, haven't you any desire to spend a day in Paris?"

"I'll go when you return."

"Why don't you go first. With my cut cheek, I would upset the family. And then, what can I do, deprived of all my charms, in the city of light?"

"You know, if you absolutely don't want to . . ."

"OK, OK, I'm going . . . . . . . . . . . . . . . . . . . . . . . .

. . . . . . . . . . . . . . . . . . . . . . . . . . . . . . . . . . . . . . . . . . . .

and the return.


. . . May. These last three days, patrols and minor brushes with the Boches.

This morning, take off with Cavel and Sagny.

At 12,500 feet over Beine, suddenly 500 feet below us, two planes. We don't know where they come from, a spontaneous apparition.

They are single-seaters, pointed wings swept back toward the rear; crosses very obvious, the classic aspect of the Boche. They fly one behind the other, taking it easy. They haven't spotted us. That one for me! The one on the right. I say to myself:

"My friend, don't panic, think, control your nerves. You have first choice! Go to it! Have to make a correction. Get him to fall in your sights. He gets bigger. You see the pilot with his black helmet. Wait, don't fire, he is not close enough; not yet, not yet, a little longer . . . Fire!"

The lever jumps before my eyes, a spurt of tracer bullets and the Boche suddenly veers off to the left; he turns on himself, there he is spinning, he descends, he falls. A slender trail of smoke. The plane, very small way down there, crashes in a wood and burns.

A victory, a victory for me alone, certain, complete. Victory toward which my will, my efforts have been directed for so long, in the course of so many combats.

Is that all there is to it? The fight was short, I met not the slightest resistance, I attacked and immediately it was finished.

Why is it that every wish fulfilled leaves a twinge of disappointment, a pinch of ashes? Still it is the major who offers felicitations, the chief who congratulates me sincerely, the comrades who shake my hand, make me a little hero, saying, "You very well deserve it!"

Elsewhere also, there will be some emotion when I write; but their joy will be tempered.

One I know will think:

"Lord, he is going to be over-confident, he will want to knock down others and will expose himself more and more . . ."

My mother will think:

"Such dangers! and then, he killed that man, I would have liked it better if he had made him prisoner."

And my father will lift his eyes to the sky, disillusioned about the prudence of his son, and will sigh and say nothing.

. . . May. The Boche of Chalons has been mousetrapped, if you'll pardon the expression.

The group has been given several super-charged Spads. They are Spads similar to ours, but having a 140 Hispano beefed up, which gives 190 or 200 hp. It is not a sewing machine; with that crate you can climb to 9000 feet in nine or ten minutes and it stays solidly in the air at over 12,000 instead of falling off in slides as with a 140. On take off, the crate tears itself away and climbs like an elevator. What a machine!

P . . . has had the first one, naturally; his co-crewman the second, so that our ace does not go out alone.

P . . . has already downed one or two Boches over the lines; but again yesterday "the Boche of Chalons" made his regular bi- or tri-weekly tour, which allowed him to slip, invulnerable, right over the group at fifteen or eighteen thousand feet.

At noon then, this choice two-seater was going quietly toward its usual objective when, suddenly, "tac-tac-tac", and the Boche began to tumble, flew to pieces, his debris covering the ground for half a kilometer.

It was P . . . and his super charged plane.

Today, routinely, another Fritz came to do the reconnaissance his defunct comrade had to break off.

This one was knocked down living. Leroux, of the 731st, joined P . . .; the two of them wounded the pilot and observer, who did a "Kamarad" in the air and they landed behind our lines.

We have been to see the crate. A pretty Albatros two-seater, brand new, varnished and touched up, on the fuselage of which the pilot had written in large white letters "VERA," doubtless the name of his girl friend.

And, as was explained to us by a reservist assigned to guard the captive German crate: "As for pigs, there are no bigger ones than those people, lieutenants. The proof is that they write it on their airplanes."*

. . . May. Every day recently a frightful bickering takes place between Bertrand and the major.

"I have three Boches officially, give me a supercharged, you can't do otherwise."

"Agreed, you're one of the very good pilots of the group, but you're only on temporary duty with us. One fine day your army will take you back and then, goodby my deluxe crate, it will go with you, and I'll be the fall guy."

And Bertrand, deeply grieved, protests, and this business of taxis makes a great fuss.

Finally the major, seeing him so downcast, says:

"Since this puts you in such a state, go get me a 180 at the annex, but only because it's you."

The next day, Bertrand brought his racing plane and the mechanics got to work on it to verify and tune up the motor, mount the machine gun, and put everything in order.

Yesterday, he tried out his machine, made a tour at 3000 feet, performed a few stunts, landed, and declared that it runs like a charm.

This morning he took, off, all alone.

I am writing in the tent when I hear some shouts outside:

"The Boche of Chalons! Ah! the dirty devil!

*A play on words: the French *verrat* means a male pig.

If P . . . was flying! Cannon shots! Just as well spit in the air . . ." etc.

I go out and finally distinguish the Fritz in the distance, an imperceptible point which speeds towards the south without being bothered by a few stray explosions.

A sudden cry, "Another crate, a crate which attacks!" and the chattering of machine guns.

The whole group is on the field, noses in the air or looking through binoculars.

"The Frenchman returns to the attack again and again. Ah! three times! four times!"

This excited clamoring crowd, has the collective and brutal soul of spectators at a Roman circus.

"There's one of them diving! The Boche!—No, the Frenchman.—Yes, the Boche! He's had it! He's a dead duck!" Then a great "Aah!—He's on fire!"

Something black breaks away from the stricken plane, whirls, falls alone in the void; it is one of the passengers. The Boche plane drops, trailing behind it a cloud of smoke. After a long fall, it crashes at four or five kilometers from the field with a deafening noise which reaches us.

A Spad drops down toward the field; at 1500 feet it does a barrel roll, a loop, two turns of a spin, lands. The pilot lifts his arms, it's Bertrand! We run, we shout, we surround him, the major shakes his hands and helps him out of his machine.

Victory Roll at Chalons

# XII

. . . 12 May. Six twenty-five. We took off at four-forty, at the break of day still grey and cold; we have had enough, we are about to quit. For the twentieth time I look at my watch. Still five minutes to go.

Low patrol; Chelcher sways near me. A while ago we had a short fight with a two-seater which fled without asking for combat; except for that incident, nothing has troubled our sortie.

My companion passes very close. I am about to give him the sign to return. Just at this instant, something passes over Suippe, toward Saint-Masmes, ten kilometers from us. Two enemy planes.

I wobble my wings. The Boches are flying southwest; they disappear for an instant, blending with the dark background of the woods; again we see them near Berru; they turn to the left and fly straight in the direction of Beine, toward our lines. They are at 4500, we are at 6000.

For an instant I study the approaching enemy, who has not seen us—two big two-seaters, slow, heavy, with large fuselages rounded underneath. But the biggest Boches are not the meanest . . .

Already Chelcher drops on the first one. Go to it! I dive on the second.

I fall on the crate and give him a burst. I am very close, my bullets should reach the target; is he going to burn, go into a tail spin, to fall?

No.

I see the passenger standing in his turret, he is not easing off; while the pilot hurries toward the ground, he fires at me with a machine gun from which spurts a double flame.

A bank, I pass beneath. I fire again; the Boche dives, he still does not want to fall or to burn. Following each other, we rapidly lose altitude; here is Beine, 2000 feet below. I'll have to let this Fritz go, this magnificent Fritz I thought was mine!

One last time. I am behind the Boche and above, in his line of fire. My machine gun fires, the twin answers it, white flakes explode to right and left. A direct hit in the fuselage and a shock under my foot; a bullet has passed under my rudder bar; the surprise makes me do a turn to the right and at the same time something stings my arm and paralyzes it; I let go of my stick and my machine gun trigger. I've been hit.

A second of sudden chill. My left hand quickly takes the place of my right and I bank with a kick of my foot to break off this nasty fight. Always with one arm, I push the throttle. I am at 1500 feet near Beine; our trenches are three or four kilometers away. Luckily my motor catches; I fly toward the lines without worrying about the Boche who has made an about face and who fires on me from behind. From the ground shots from rifles, machine guns and cannon. Pushing at full power, 1600 rpm, suddenly a burst makes me jump; the second Boche bars the route and fires with his two Maxims. This time, I'm in a real scrape! Wounded, at 1500 feet over the enemy lines, I'm still forced to fight and maneuver with one hand! Provided that I receive nothing in my motor or my propeller!

But a plane falls like a whirlwind on my adversary, fires, turns around him. The Fritz lets me go to defend himself against Chelcher, who arrives in the nick of time to get me out of this brawl.

The lines . . .

I reduce speed, my right arm rests limp on my knee, my fingers are stretched out and stiff, my wrist is warm and sticky with blood; the pain, nothing a while ago, starts to throb in my arm, which must be broken.

I would very much like to be on the ground, but if I land here, in this no man's land, I will flip over in a shell hole or will be left in the lurch, without help for I don't know how long. I must get back to the field.

I gain a little height. Chelcher, who cannot know that I am hit, passes near me, says hello and does a couple of stunts.

I am very tired. I take off my glove, my hand is already covered with dried blood, while a dark thread drips from each of my fingers. I would look at my wound, but when I try to lift my sleeve it hurts me, and I have to fly. I've had enough . . .

The field . . .

I land with my left hand, not too badly, and out of pride, I roll to the Bessonneaus. I stop my Spad quite near to Chelcher.

"Well, mon lieutenant, it didn't work out with that big bird?"

But he interrupts himself when he sees how bad I look, jumps from his crate, calls, and comrades run to help me get out of my seat.

I can stand up very well. I walk with short steps to the car, and twenty minutes later, supported by Lamajou, I am in the hospital at Chalons.

My friend holds my hand while they put me to sleep on a white table; also as I wake up, my mouth full of ether, in a room too hot, in which they do not want to open the window; he stays near me, listens to my story, wipes my forehead with a fresh handkerchief, and gives me brotherly encouragement.

And then, after all, if I am sick at my stomach, if my arm in its cast is very heavy, I still feel that there is nothing very serious. Tomorrow things will be better, in a month I will fly. I think that fate has again extended my term.

The hospital.

A large bright room, twelve beds, a woman admirably active and silent. Fever and pain.

Not a word, except a few moans and a few calls.

Eleven badly wounded, and myself admitted here by favor. Seven infantrymen, Zouves, chasseurs, foot-sloggers; two artillerymen; three aviators.

The light and the torpor of noon weigh on us and tire us. Madame de C . . .* moves noiselessly, watches over everything, while two women, mothers of those who are the worst wounded, watch and wait without a movement and without a word.

Dressings, bandaged heads, limbs tight in plaster, wounds still open which have constantly to be washed, raised beds where aching legs are protected from contact with the sheets.

There are pitiful faces because they are too young, others lamentable because they are already old; impassible faces, or frightened, or tense, and others empty of all expression, as if their spirits had been darkened by fatigue and suffering.

A wounded skeleton seems barely to be alive, a young school teacher. He is ravaged, aged, bald.

*Madame de Coligny, descendant of Admiral de Coligny, assassinated at the massacre of St. Bartholomew—an admirable woman. J. B. V.

[246]

In bed for eight months, he cannot be transported, paralyzed by a shell fragment in the spinal cord.

A Saint-Cyrian of nineteen has an arm cut off.

Savas, a lawyer from Nice, has an arm and leg crushed and a bullet in his stomach. He grimaces continually, tortured, while his neighbor seems to see nothing, to think nothing, to feel nothing. This is Regalat, a vine-grower from the Midi. They have cut off his foot; he is still astonished at the disaster of his amputation, stunned, frightened.

The artilleryman is a big fellow of thirty; he has the distant air of a boy of good family brought up by the Jesuits. All day long, with eyes obstinately raised to the ceiling, he dreams, taciturn. They have cut off his leg at the thigh.

On the right, Captain Grand moans from time to time; he is a squadron chief of forty-five, father of four children; he has flown like a young man, he has had a serious crash. Six fractures (leg, ribs, pelvis) keep him here, stretched out, suffering like a martyr.

Three days ago they brought a pilot of a three-seater into the room. They think he is going to die. In combat an explosive shell struck him, splitting his knee. He had, however, the energy to bring back the heavy R.4 from Pont-Faverger to our lines, saving his observer and his machine gunner, both badly hit. His fever constantly rises, his mother is near him.

Motionless and pale, he is so handsome that the wounded who surround him, though so little in condition to see and to wonder, are astonished into silence. His neighbor, especially, marvels and is sad. He is an adjutant of the Zouaves, with grey hair. A retired non-commissioned officer, he left the postal service in Algeria to take a section. Looking at the pilot, he forgets his own pain and his broken shoulder.

There are still others . . .

Hot air, the stale smell of bandages, the anxiety, the fever. Each is preoccupied, silent, and alone with his close companion, suffering.

The evening brings a moment of freshness and of relaxation, a short respite, which precedes the tension of the night. The wounded speak.

Savas, the lawyer, kids. Between two grimaces, he makes awful puns on detestable words and teases the girl aide, Mlle Eugénie, who answers with tears in her eyes, for she is compassionate . . . Captain Grand speaks of his children to the artilleryman, father of a little girl. Madame de C . . . , who, in taking care of so many poor soldiers, has lost the feeling for small proprieties, while maintaining a proper sense of proportion, discusses gravely with Segalat the characteristics of the pou, or head louse, and the cootie, or body louse.

A lieutenant, whose name I don't know, an unpretentious fellow, thinks back on the people he has known, his neighbors, friends, employers, those of his district or profession, counts the young men who have shirked their duty and have escaped the heavy price he has paid to the limit of his strength and beyond.

"It's frightful how many of them have landed cushy jobs," he concludes, and turns over moaning.

The Saint-Cyrian tells of the taking of Mont-Haut. One would think it was a canto from *The Inferno*. The battle returns in memory and he grows excited in reliving it.

All this confusion of voices makes the pilot, Minori, nervous and tired; yet Madame de C . . .

doesn't dare quiet the wounded, for this moment of relaxation distracts and comforts them.

Day before yesterday evening, they brought a tattered human here, an infantryman whose skull had been fractured. He died during the night.

Heavy hours, distressing hours, but how fertile, those passed here! Now everything is clear to me, all is simple. I have recovered the scale of value which will allow me to measure the actions and the character of men, to determine my own duty.

At the front, action takes nearly every moment, it scarcely gives us time to think; we do our task without regard to the effort of those around us. In the rear, bluff and lies pervert our judgment. But here one sees clearly.

We can see the shocking inequality of the sacrifices.

We can see that he who has given only time and mental labor has given nothing to his country compared to him who has given himself, his mortal body and suffering flesh.

What a chasm separates "serving" and "rendering services"! From the material point of view, they may be equal; from the moral point of view, the one is noble, the other commonplace; the one is the act of the soldier, the other of the bureaucrat.

Finally here each one is given his due: admiration, indifference or contempt.

The only great, the only real sacrifice is that of those mysterious things, profound, sacred—our life, our suffering, our flesh.

Only those who will have seen personal combat, who will have held a gun, a machine gun, serviced a piece, only those who will have been under fire, will be able to say:

"On us has weighed the terrible burden of the war. We have given something to our country, we have proved to it our love in effective and real fashion.

"And we knew the value of that which we gave, we knew the danger; we were not the young soldiers of the beginning of the war. We had seen the harrowing sight of wounded men, of unforgettable deaths. Almost all of us had been wounded and still we returned to the danger of combat of our own free will, because we felt it was our duty. On us, on our effort, our sufferings, our pain, rests the whole destiny of the nation."

Let those who have given their country only their mental labor, their work, and their time have their modest place and rank. Could they give less in this war where our national life is engaged? Certainly, there are specialists who must be left their specialties, for the general interest demands it, but for goodness sake, judge these workers on their merits; do not compare them with soldiers.

As for those who have no valid excuse for evading payment of the price of blood, it is here, in the domain of suffering, where we can judge them, where we can understand how great is their slackness and their baseness.

The young and healthy who become office workers, road builders, chauffeurs, pen pushers, station masters, bookkeepers, or counted the oil cans during the battles of the Marne, the Yser and Verdun; those whose posts are out of cannon range, who, jovial and freshly shaved, watch muddy artillerymen and infantrymen wearily

Salute to Valour

trudging into battle; .........................
............................................
............................................
Those who will profit from victory without
having suffered; ............................. .
............................................
............................................
Young men who have let Captain Grand, already old, serve in their place; educated men,
from the managerial class, who have allowed
Regalat, simple and slow, to command a unit;
vigorous and healthy men, who have seen Minori,
exempted on account of bad health and enfeebled,
join up and fight; such as these should be con-
demned by all Frenchmen.

One should ...............................
............................................
............................................
............................................
Silent hours, full of pain and tumultuous
thoughts.

The doctor makes his rounds, feels the pulse,
looks at the faces.

"Do you feel better?" . . . "Not much."

Then, Madame de C . . . , devoted and un-
tiring shadow:

"Why don't you go to sleep?"

"I can hear the cannon."

"But no! No!"

When one is wounded, one cannot forget the
great misery of war; it continues, always more
severe, for the comrades at the front.

"Good by, old boy! We'll see you in three
weeks!"

"Say hello to Paris for me!"

"Try to get your arm back in shape."

"Find a corner seat in the train!"

"At least come back! Don't fall into an ambush —the road is dangerous."

"Don't worry about anything."

"Well, in three weeks, our little expedition, mon lieutenant?"

"In three weeks, good by chief! Good by, Lamajou, old boy! Good by Chelcher, tried and true!" And convalescence.

Paris.—At the front, the atmosphere of battle entirely dominates us. The German is an adversary. But here, it is hate which surrounds us. Hate of the Boche, no longer the adversary, but the enemy.

Hate in memory of what the country has risked, the odious attack, the ignoble acts, the misery of the invaded regions, the useless bombardments, the martyrdom of prisoners, the destruction of all the beauties and of all the refinements. Hate which is sustained by the continuing daily losses of dearest friends. As long as I live, these unjust, iniquitous, inexpiable deaths will oppress my thoughts.

And then, there are other painful things—the anguish of my father and my sister. My mother who has suffered more than it is possible to imagine.

All of this hate will help me to go back, when the time comes. For there are still the Boches over the lines. That is a situation a bit ignored here, and which should be more known.

# XIII

. . . 28 June. "Good by. When will you come back?"

"Before three months, surely."

"Three months!"

"Go, leave now, that will be better for us all."

"Au revoir! . . ."

In the train Flippe, returning from seven days leave; Sagny, who had had forty-eight hours. We talk, and in a second that which I have left at Paris is already far away; I am again "at the front"; have I ever left it?

The wagon restaurant full of horizon-blue uniforms.

Returned to our compartment, we discuss our air combats.

"Do you know what's happened to the group?"

"Yes, they wrote to me—a little. I didn't answer, didn't have time."

In a corner, a Captain of the Alpines drowses; he wakes at the noise of our conversation, speaks of the last hard blows at Laffaux and Chemin des Dames. Then we begin to banter. Paris—The Captain takes fire.

"Paris! Ah! oui Paris, only let's talk of it! I'm just coming back, and I've never seen it so well

. . . . . . . . . . . . . . . . . . . . . . . . . . . . . . . . . . . . . . . . . . . . . .

. . . . . . . . . . . . . . . . . . . . . . . . . . . . . . . . . . . . . . . . . . . . . .

. . . . . . . . . . . . . . . . . . . . . . . . . . . . . . . . . . . . . . . . . . . . . .

. . . . . . . . . . . . . . . . . . . . . . . . . . . . . . . . . . . . . . . . .

"Formerly we were borne up by a clear and joyous flame. Now disillusioned pride upholds us:

the pride of being' us', those who will not give way, those who will hold out, those on whom rests the existence of the nation. ..................

.............................................

.............................................

.............................................

Chalons!

Lamajou and Chelcher are at the station and I jump into the old Pan-Pan.

"How do you feel now?"

"Still going strong, comme le whisky."*

"And your arm?"

"Half and half."*

"Well go-gone, as Octave says. It wasn't too hard to leave Paris?"

"A little, but I never stopped thinking of the day I would have to return; so the end of my leave did not seem a catastrophe to me. And then, you know, a man has to be wounded and deprived of his crate to know how much he loves to fly."

"And your parents?"

"They know how to bear up; the bad advice comes especially from those who have something to be ashamed of. Certain people said to me innocently, 'You have done enough.' Others, less delicate, have identified my mentality with theirs; 'Now that you have everything that you want, the Croix, citations, why do you want to go back?'

"The rear has given me the blues; now, that's over. How can one be blue here? Just being with you again restores my good spirits and my nerve. Let's go to the intelligence tent."

Under the tent, the chiefs, gathered around the major, have a perplexed air.

*These sentences stand as in the original text.

"What's wrong?"

"The group is leaving."

"Where to?"

"Up north. Dunkirk, someplace up there, a country *en beck, en inghe or en boom*."*

"When?"

"Don't know; five or six days maybe."

"We shouldn't worry about it. Dunkirk! We'll swim; there must be some sea planes there. It will be funny to attack these barges and to see the Boche sink and drown in the sea."

"Let's go!" growls Bertrand. "Anyway, the first thing *I* have to do is see about my rolling stock. The north is a long way off."

Chelcher stays with me.

I ask him to tell me what the squadron has been up to during my absence.

"And Piston, what's happened to Piston?"

"Piston! Poor devil, who will ever know? You remember how excitable he was. He got into his flying togs one morning saying, 'This time I'm going to get one!' Sagny was to have gone with him, but his motor wouldn't start. Piston left, alone. He was never seen again."

"Nothing was ever learned?"

"Nothing, neither from the balloons, nor from the observation posts; nothing. Pfutt! Gone up in thin air. It left a terrible void in the squadron. He was a nervy fellow, amazing, never tired, excellent pilot. It was a great shock to us to see him disappear like that. Only with time, you know—it's terrible how we forget the best ones!"

*The syllables *beck (beke), inghe (inge)* appear in the names of several towns of this region, all in Belgium: Moerbeke, Harlebeke, Meulebeke, Roosebeke; Poperinghe (Poperinge) is southeast of Dunkirk; the town Boom lies between Brussels and Antwerp.

"Haven't there been other losses?"

"Yes, the lieutenant who replaced you. A dragoon, fine guy, but a bit young in the trade. Name of Colet. He took off one morning on patrol with de Loris; they attacked a single-seater near Nauroy. The Fritz started to zig zag to shake them off. We don't know exactly what happened; the Boche must have done too brisk a turn; he flew into Colet, who was going full speed.

"The two crates slammed together. Pieces flew everywhere and everything crashed to the ground."

"And who replaced Colet?"

"A lieutenant of light troops, Lanier. Nothing great, pale and white livered; he let spider webs gather on his crate, indeed, your old Spad, with its black pennants. That didn't go over well at all with the boss who bridles at what's contrary to his idea of a fight. He hasn't had any of that for a long time. Get going! get going! to the schools, or some technical dump, or the hydros, or America. We saw him leave one morning, his valise in his hand."

"And have we shot down any Fritz?"

"We haven't done so bad. Sagny got his second, the captain and Cavel together cooled one off at the other end of the sector, almost to the Argonne. Divergnes knocked down a two-seater and Legrand another, but it wasn't confirmed, lack of witnesses."

"Well, I'm going to have to get back in practice. Why shouldn't I succeed like the other boys? Meanwhile, the boss has given me a super-charged . . ."

# XIV

*Blemshoote.**

. . . July. This is a dismal country. We have
not seen any hydroplanes. We have not strolled
the beaches in white flannels and straw hats. As
for baths, we take one each evening when we
slip between our sheets, for the tent in which we
sleep is so damp that they seem still wet from the
wash.

In addition, plenty of fighting.

Escort missions to hell and gone to protect
range finding, lengthy flights in formation, and
Fritz who are not children and who show themselves to be very aggressive.

The voyage went off well; a stop at Bourget,
then the arrival here on a good field whose only
defect is that it is swept every other day by wind
from the sea, violent enough to upset the taxis
and to blow away the Bessonneaus.

I am getting back in the routine of flying fast
enough. I had lost a good bit of my sharpness
during six weeks of inaction; now I am back in the
groove and I feel comfortable in my supercharged,
which is, however, a bit different from the 140.

I teased a few Fritz. I awaited my first combat
with much impatience and a little nervousness.
But it went off very well; neither nervousness
nor anxiety. I had to deal with two single-seaters
who ended up by giving way. I looked calmly at
the serpentine paths of their incendiaries. (Need
I say that they fired like bunglers?) I even thought

---

*This and other fictitious Flemish place names serve to
disguise the remaining incidents of the narrative. Lieutenant
Villars did not fly on the Flanders front.

I had one of them, but after having dived three hundred feet or so, he straightened out and regained altitude.

For the rest, the 705th is always what it was, gay, lively, perfectly in shape.



. . . July. Always up to our ears in hard and not very amusing work; escorts of two-seaters at high altitudes where the Fritz does not come looking for us, or else patrols of numerous planes in tight formation which sweep the sky before them.

When the day is not too full, we go off by ourselves, groups of two or three in what we call "productive flights" with the sole purpose of destroying the Boche. That has already produced some results. Hatfield, an American who joined us recently, grilled a two-seater a few days after his arrival at the front. When he landed and wanted to tell us about his victory, the little French he knew got lost in emotion and no one could understand what he was trying to explain.

Legrand and Meceni have also knocked down a plane; they were protecting a G.6 when an unobservant two-seater flew 600 feet below them. They dived on him one after the other and wiped him out before he knew what hit him.

The rest is hours of flight, endless and tedious. The altitude exhausts me. I don't eat, I don't smoke, I sleep badly, I don't have the heart to read or to write; I am like an adding machine in totaling up patrols, missions, and cover flights.



. . . July. A tough encounter. Alone with Chelcher, six kilometers into Fritz territory, we were jumped by five Albatroses we had allowed to approach, taking them for Englishmen.

A great dance around us with all their Maxims; I don't know how we got out of it. A ball had gone through Chelcher's radiator and he was doing acrobatics in the midst of a cloud of white vapor; as for me, I had a respectable number of holes in my canvas, a cable cut and a strut severed. We heaved a great sigh of relief when the Boches let us go on reaching our lines.


. . . July. The quartermaster sergeant comes to find me as I get out of my plane.

"Mon lieutenant, an officer of the 783rd has telephoned you. He asks you to go see him at the G.C. 42 when you have time. It's Lieutenant Loubet, or Loupet . . ."

"Louvet! I am going to find little Lou! I saw him at Pau this winter, but I didn't know what the devil had happened to him . . ."

Two or three days later, on a rainy afternoon, I jump in the auto and speed towards Ravestraate where G.C. 42 is camped.

"The 783rd . . .?"

"Those barracks you see over there behind a Bessonneau . . ."

A pilot smokes, sitting in front of the door of the cabin. I know him, we have been at school together.

I give him a joyful hello:

"Well, Laville, are things going as you like?"

"Thanks, and you, mon lieutenant?"

"And Louvet, is he somewhere around here?"

The face of the non-commissioned officer stiffens:

"Didn't you know?"

"What?"

"Lt. Louvet was knocked down in flames, over German lines, near Clerken, yesterday morning."

What! Louvet, too! Little Lou, a friend of ten years, schoolmate, companion in the regiment and in war. In 1914 we slept on the same straw, ate from the same mess kit. In Lorraine during the first days of the war, we had charged side by side.

Under fire his was the calmest courage, the coolest, and at the same time the most enthusiastic. During the eighteen months he passed in a good squadron as observer, he did great things: special missions, reconnaisances, victorious combats. And here he is fallen, he also. I will never see him again!

I will never see him again. I can't believe it. Foolishly I ask Laville, "Are you sure?" He answers "yes" with a nod of his head.

I cannot realize that he is dead, gone, vanished. That troubles and frightens me, so much he is still alive for me. Tomorrow I'm going to see him come into my room, blond, neat, hair combed, quiet. A book under his arm, he will sit on my bed and watch me write without bothering me; or we will talk of comrades, or officers we have met during almost four years of similar existence. He seemed a bit slow, gauche and lazy, but in action and in danger his companions knew how much he could be alive, energetic, and master of himself.

"Little Lou is dead." I repeat:

"You are sure?"

"Yes, his comrades in combat saw him go down in a tail spin, burn in the air, and end by burning on the ground . . ."

"Adieu."

I go back to my auto and drive off with a sad heart.

. . . July. "The captain got another one!" Sagny lands and shouts the news. Behind him comes Bertrand who jumps out of his machine and walks around his wings looking for the possible traces of bullets. He makes a great effort to appear calm, but overflows with rage.

"If it hadn't been for those recruits, of Group D, I would have made those two Fritz land alive behind our lines: the observer was signaling 'Kamarad.' But here these little vultures arrived and began to fly around my Fritz, like a flock of crows to steal him from me. In the fight, the pilot began to run for his lines. I had to put an end to all that. Tic! Tac! the crate dived; I saw the poor machine gunner grab hold of his turret, then the whole thing tail spinned to the ground."

"Come along, mon capitaine, come to the information room to get this Boche confirmed."

Renaud tells about an encounter:

"When we say that we fly alone, strangers are at first surprised, then ask a stupid question:

"'Then you can do what you want?'

"Or, 'Aren't you bored?'

"Or again: 'Since no one is there to see you, you only fight when you feel like it!'

"Thus each bumpkin* views in his own way the difficulties and the advantages of our grim solitude.

"But our crates are not as much single-seaters

*The author uses the Annamese term *niakoué*, peasant, argot of French soldiers in Indo-China.

as people would like to believe; each carries a passenger.

"There are ferocious figure heads."

"Figure head! No, old man, how would you install it with the prop where it is?"

"It is true, we will let our friend sit on the edge of the cockpit. She will whisper in our ear. Fierce images, I've said. Certain pilots carry at their side hate of the Boche, love of combat, desire for glory, and they fly, deaf to all other voices. But there are also less tragic passengers.

"I know some whose smile is not warlike but who nevertheless give to those they accompany much comfort in fatigue and in the fray. I know some who sit faithfully by the fighters through lengthy flights, many a reconnaissance, and sharp engagement. You, don't you owe much to your passenger?"

"A lot."

"For my part," says Bertrand, "when I fly, I never think of a woman."

"What weighs on your mind, then?"

"I don't know. My motor, which purrs or doesn't purr; gas pressure, my machine gun, my oil circulation."

"A guy without poetry! You're the one who complains when we play soft music and who begs for English dances."

"Pardon! American, Sousa's marches, as far as possible."


. . . July. Day of attack. Hours of flight amidst hurtling shells.

Fallen Comrade

. . . July. More of the same.


. . . July. Cover, forays; forays, cover. These northern Boches come less often over our lines than those of Champagne, but they fight better and the combats last longer.

When we escort a reconnaissance fifteen kilometers behind enemy lines, we see the Fritz take off and climb to attack us. But since we see them from the beginning, they profit nothing, for they arrive too late or else attack us in dispersed order and are in for a disagreeable surprise.

Our English neighbors cause them serious losses. They do not have very good planes, but they fly on their patrols with an admirable discipline and with devilish courage.

From time to time they take the air fifteen or twenty at once and carry out a great sweep. The "Huns" really take a pasting from this; with each of these sorties we see three or four shot down in flames or fly to pieces.

. . . July. Yesterday, a heavy blow.

The captain left in pursuit with Legrand and Divergnes. The latter had a breakdown in pressure at the start of the patrol and had to return. The two other single-seaters continued, accompanied by a Spad from the 707th which came to join them.

At about 12,000 feet, five kilometers from our lines, they fell on two Boches single-seaters, rotary-engined crates which did not seem to be very fast.

The captain attacked one of them, but his machine gun quit with the first shots and he got out of the way to unjam it.

The Boches had not seen our comrades arrive; surprised by the detonations, one dived and disappeared; the other faced them. With a zoom he climbed to encounter Legrand, who dived on him; with a few rounds the Boche lodged a ball in his leg, then, in turning, wounded in the belly the pilot of the 707th, who arrived in his turn.

This Boche must have been an extraordinary shot. His plane, slow enough, climbed like an elevator; he maneuvered it admirably. He remained master of the field till a squadron of eighteen or twenty English came to attack him. He knocked one of the new arrivals down in flames, but overwhelmed by all these assailants, he took fire in the air a few instants later. An ace.

As for Legrand, the ball which had hit him had broken his lower leg. Crazy with pain, and losing much blood, he dived straight down, from 12,000 to the ground, and landed in the first opening which presented itself.

With a dead prop he landed in a marsh, five kilometers from the front lines; his Spad flipped over in the muddy water. Only with great difficulty did he escape drowning and succeed in unbuckling himself, clinging to his plane, getting out of the mud, and dragging his poor broken leg, lying down on the wing of his plane to wait for help.

It was only two hours later that some artillerymen, walking in water up to their chests, came to carry him away and put him in an ambulance.

A few minutes later they cut off his leg at the thigh, in fear of gangrene which, following his immersion, had already reached his knee.

The captain, Sagny and I have been to see him, the same evening. Bertrand cried like a child in giving him the medaille militaire and in giving him the accolade. Legrand was as brave as he could possibly be. This big, handsome boy who had just had an amputation spoke only of his comrades, his joy in knowing that his chief was safe and sound, and his sadness in leaving us.*

. . . August. The chief got another Boche. A two-seater which burned in the air and whose debris fell on the front lines.

. . . August. We take off together, Chelcher, Loris and I, all three flying supercharged planes. At 15,000 feet we cruise from the forest of Houthulst to the sea. The ground is almost hidden by the morning fog which the sun is only starting to dissipate. Over the lines, no one.

We have been airborne for an hour. Chelcher waggles his Spad; four single-seaters are coming toward us—Albatroses; they are grouped, flying straight ahead; they haven't seen us.

At the first glance we recognize that they are Boches: camouflaged by asymmetric bands, dark green, yellow and brown, they have the appearance of vultures with irregular spotted wings;

*The incident about Legrand (his real name) is exactly as related to me by Captain Derode when he visited me in the hospital. A few months later Captain Derode was killed. J. B. V.

[271]

their thick fuselages, wings in V, short noses, motley color, sinister crosses give them an indescribably doubtful and malignant air. They approach.

For me! I attack the last one, the straggler. He is very close, I fire, I am going to get him; he dives straight down, I only have to follow him; but his comrades at the noise of the machine gun, suddenly turn, face me, surround me, and I am obliged to let loose of my adversary to defend myself.

In his turn, Loris attacks. He drops like an arrow behind an Albatros, a burst of fire leaves his Vickers and the Boche seems to blow up in the air; the wings come off the fuselage, fly in pieces, multicolored on one side, grey on the other, while the body of the plane and its motor tumble earthward.

The two other single-seaters dive full speed and disappear. We complete the foray and we go home.

We surround de Loris, we shake his hand. Can a pilot carry off a more complete and brilliant victory? We accompany him to the intelligence room where again he is admired and congratulated.

As for my Boche, no observer saw him fall, and we were too occupied with our combat to follow him with our eyes. Thus he is lost for me. I hope that my bullets were not lost for him.

Chelcher grumbles a bit. His machine gun was jammed and he could not take part in the fight.

"Come along, old man, don't let it worry you; the next time it will be our turn, yours or mine."

. . . Pilot Lieutenant X . . . , of the N705 disappeared, the 6 August 1917, on the Flanders front, in the course of an aerial combat.

The Hawk

# Index

The original French edition was without an index. The translators have here supplied one for the convenience of readers.

Tracts, scattered over German
lines, 43
Troyon, place, 65
Tunis, 184 n.

Vadelaincourt, flying field,
23, 37; in June, 1916, 41;
58, 59, 63; stormy night at,
68; visitors to, 71; 97, 100;
hospital at, 112
Valkyries, 165
Vacherauville, place, 87, 96;
fort, 117, 127
Vauquois, place, 23
Vaux, pool of, 31; locality of,
57; fort, 66, 117, 120 (blown
up), 123, 124 (carried)
Vera, "verrat," play on words,
239
Verdun, 21, 23; view from air,
31 ff.; range finding over,
37; Farman shot down over,
38; German offensive of
June 1916, 58 ff.; 68; Russian cannon at, 81; low
flight over, 85; morale of
army at, 96; French offensive of October 1916, 117 ff.;
freed, 124; further French
offensive of December 1916,
125 ff.; 201, 209, 250
Vickers, machine gun, 143,
163, 272
Villars, Jean Beraud, arrives
May 17, 1916, at Verdun
front, 23; first sees Verdun
front from the air, 31; first
range finding over Ver-
dun, 37; goes on liaison to
Army Corps headquarters,
39; flies an artillery spotting
mission with Delame, 41;
engages two enemy planes
with Basil, 46; with Basil
has brief encounter with
enemy plane, 51; goes with
Max to photograph new

German emplacements, 60;
with Delame tests the ceiling of his new 130 hp Farman, 64 ff.; shares room
with Max in Adrian hut,
70-71; goes on liaison to
various headquarters with
his commander (Capt. Par-
direl) and Peyrussac, 72 ff.;
his feeling for flying, 77;
makes low flight over Verdun, 85-87; flies photo-
graphic mission with Del-
ame, accompanied by Max
and Carrier, 88; attacked by
German plane, 88; flies
trainees, 97; attitude toward
trainees, 97; goes to Bar-le-
Duc and then Chalons for
new plane, 100; sees cap-
tured German fliers at
Chalons, 107; does artillery
spotting with Max, 118;
sees fort at Douaumont
blown up, 119-20; flies in
French offensive of October
24, 1916, but lost in fog,
121-22; flies again same
evening over zone of Ger-
man retreat, likened to
Dante's Inferno, 123-24;
watches French troops moving up preparatory to the
attack of December 1916,
125-26; flies with Max in
the attack of December 15,
1916, 126-27; sees long lines
of German prisoners, 129;
leaves Verdun to join a pursuit squadron, 130; arrives
at Lépinois airfield to join
a squadron of Nieuports,
137; gets lost flying over
Compiègne, 140; machine
gun jams in combat, 143;
flies in snowstorm, 150-51;
attacks enemy plane, 157,

163; face frozen on high flight, 176; attacks enemy plane, 187; secures surrender of German plane in the air, 225; forced landing from motor failure, 226; shoots down enemy plane, 236-37; wounded in air combat, 244; in hospital, 245 ff.

Visitors to the flying field, attitude toward, 71

Voisin, French plane, 22, 24, 37, 49

Walpurgis night, 165

*War Birds: Diary of an Unknown Aviator*, 164 n.

"Wechsel," German direction sign in Noyon, 166

Woman's stocking, as amulet, 154, 185 n., 221

Yser, river, 92, 250

Zouaves, 85, 112, 129, 229, 234, 247

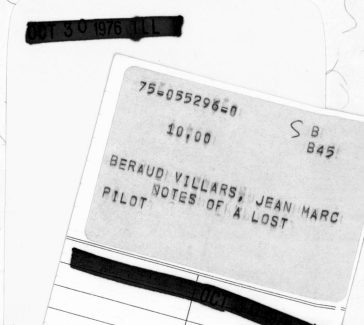